"Laurie Hall's book offers hope, heart, and the Lord's healing to readers who have experienced relational betrayal. She takes an honest and biblical look at the sin that invades our lives and the forgiveness process that restores us. She doesn't sugar-coat anything—not life, sin, pain, or the forgiveness process. But through courageous sharing of her own experiences, she invites us to walk with Jesus in the reality of our disappointments."

JERRY R. KIRK

Chairman and CEO, National Coalition for the Protection of Children & Families

"This book is a treasury of spiritual insights and strategies. Chapter three is worth the price of the book alone. For a cutting edge book that will renew families, *The Cleavers Don't Live Here Anymore* is a prudent choice."

KEN CANFIELD, Ph.D.

Founder and President, National Center for Fathering

"Many Christians will tell a wounded husband or wife to forgive his or her spouse, but they provide no workable 'tools' to help with the process. In this book, Laurie gives us honest, practical steps and provides a unique perspective on the whole area of forgiveness. Laurie promises that through prayer and a new spiritual outlook we will be led to the higher ground of righteousness and blessing. I highly recommend this book."

ANITA WORTHEN

Author, *Someone I Love Is Gay*
Founder, New Hope Ministries

"Laurie Hall has first-hand experience with pain and disillusionment, and she has seen abuse perpetuated in the name of the Church. Without offering glib formulas, her thought-provoking book shows the difference that a true Christian response can make when serious sin, such as adultery and pornography, destroys marriage and family."

JOHN W. KENNEDY

World News Editor, *Pentecostal Evangel*

"As president of a law firm that has helped hundreds of cities fight pornography, I have seen its devastating influence on communities. *The Cleavers Don't Live Here Anymore* goes beyond the reach of law to give a prescription for healing that families afflicted by pornography desperately need."

SCOTT D. BERGTHOLD

President, Community Defense Counsel

P9-CAM-272

Also by Laurie Hall:

An Affair of the Mind
One woman's courageous battle
to salvage her family from the
devastation of pornography

The Cleavers Don't Live Here Anymore

Bringing Hope and Radical Forgiveness
to the Bewilderment, Betrayal,
and Bitterness of Real Family Life

LAURIE SHARLENE HALL

SERVANT PUBLICATIONS
ANN ARBOR, MICHIGAN

© 2000 by Laurie Hall
All rights reserved.

Vine Books is an imprint of Servant Publications especially designed to serve evangelical Christians.

Scripture verses, unless other noted, are from the King James Version. Verses marked AMPLIFIED are from the Amplified Bible. Old Testament ©1965, 1987 by the Zondervan Corporation. The Amplified New Testament ©1958, 1987 by the Lockman Foundation. Used by permission.

To protect the privacy of the individuals whose stories are told in this book, most names and characterizations have been fictionalized, although they are based on real events.

Published by Servant Publications
P.O. Box 8617
Ann Arbor, Michigan 48107

Cover design: Left Coast Design, Portland, Oregon

00 01 02 03 10 9 8 7 6 5 4 3 2 1

Printed in the United States of America
ISBN 1-56955-131-6

LIBRARY OF CONGRESS CATALOGING-IN-PUBLICATION DATA

Hall, Laurie Sharlene.
The Cleaver's don't live here anymore : bringing hope and radical forgiveness to the bewilderment, betrayal, and bitterness of real family life / Laurie Sharlene Hall.
    p.   cm.
Includes bibliographical references.
ISBN 1-56955-131-6 (alk. paper)
1. Married persons—Religious life. 2. Marriage—Religious aspects—Christianity.   I. Title.
BV4596.M3 H35 2000
248.4—dc21   99-088896

To
Gammie and Gampie

for cherry cough drops
and
cuckoo clocks
and
snuggles and giggles and sweet petunias
and
for hanging to the riggings—*No Matter What*

Contents

Humming, Faintly
by Laurie Hall

I look for answers.
He offers a Way.

I think in terms of destination.
He speaks in terms of Path.

I ask about the present.
He whispers of the Presence.

I rage over troubles without.
He calls me to Peace within.

I wallow in fear.
He consumes with Love.

I cry out, "The darkness! The darkness overtakes me!"
He says, "My child, don't you know the Light of the World shines within?"

Shine, therefore, O Light Within.
Brighten the Way.
Illuminate the Path.
Show me the Presence.
Picture the Peace.
Reveal the Love.
Teach me to hum, however faintly, in the darkness
Knowing the Light of the World lives within.

Acknowledgments

Y ou know the difference between commitment and involvement, don't you? It's like the difference between bacon and eggs. The chicken is involved but the pig is committed.

My name is on the cover of this book as author. I was committed (and nearly so) to the work of the book, but others were involved in helping me write it and they deserve a few cock-a-doodle-doos.

I have a wonderful board of directors who not only listened endlessly to my thoughts, but also designed prayer guides, licked stamps, and stuffed envelopes to coordinate the 100 or so folks who prayed for this book. Larry and Ann Murphy, Bart and Kathy Farley, Jim and Joanne Foote, Steve and Judy Barone—you're the best!

I wish I could thank them all, but space does not permit the listing of all those who regularly pray for me and this ministry. Besides, if I listed a hundred names or more, it would make this read like the begats and then your eyes would begin to glaze over and I'd lose you. However, there are some people who pray for me on a daily or several times a week basis and it only seems right to tell you about them. Diana Kriesel is my wall woman, daily surrounding me in prayer. Kevin Flierl coordinates a prayer effort for this ministry among the men at Moody Bible Institute. Barb Platting has now amazingly prayed me through two books. Yami Morgan is one wild, howling woman and her prayers have saved me more times than I can tell. My dear friends Sister Marie Catherine and Sister Patricia have graced my life with both hospitality and prayer. Near the end of the book, my sisters-in-law, Jane and Barbie, undertook fasting and prayer for both Steve and me and their prayers did amazing things. My matchless longtime friends, Mark and Sharon Brook, Lyn Steriti, Paul and Arlene Marquis, and Jim and Teresa Quinn provided both prayer and ballast. Thanks also to Scott and Teresa Masdon for their hard work editing *There's Hope*, the new magazine of my ministry, The Elijah Initiative, which I initiated in response to the outpouring of reader correspondence from *An Affair of the Mind. There's Hope* is available to anyone who writes the address in the back of this book.

I know there are others, because I feel their prayers. Unfortunately, I don't know all their names, but God does. Their prayers are powerful, and if you are blessed by anything in this book, know that in God's ledger book, the prayer warriors get big-time credit for it.

Speaking of prayer, my wonderful editor Kathy Deering not only prayed and coordinated prayer for this book, she cheered it out of me. Kathy, Bert Ghezzi, Gwen Ellis, and the other great folks at Servant Publications believed in this project and gave it amazing time and attention.

Thanks also are due Rev. Henry MacLeod, rector of St. James Episcopal Church, for his willingness to lend insight into chapter 18 of Matthew. And to Henri Nouwen, who coined the phrase "Hope is humming in the darkness," which continues to haunt me with its grace and courage and which formed the basis for the poem that opens this book.

Tim and Kathy VonDuyke and Janet Franklin were terrific sounding boards for some of the concepts in this book. Becky was an extraordinary listener. In addition, I am so grateful for the hundreds of men and women who have shared their stories with me and whose wisdom, courage, and perseverance I highly respect.

Most of the zippy phrases in this book come from my warped little mind, but a few came via the World Wide Web. "Change is inevitable, except from a vending machine," "Some drink at the fountain of knowledge, others only gargle," "The gates are down, the lights are flashing, but the train is nowhere in sight," and "Dust: Mud with the juice squeezed out" were on various e-mails sent by some cubicle-dweller with way too much free time. There were no attributions given and I was the zillionth person on the "Mail to:" list, so I can't give credit where credit is due. Whoever you are out there in cyberland, thanks!

Finally, I thank my family, who have taught me so much and encouraged me to persevere. The Cleavers didn't live at our house. We are still, as a card someone once gave me said:

UNDER CONSTRUCTION
This is the future site of a perfect family.
Currently, however, it is under mental, physical, and spiritual construction.
Inquiries concerning inconveniences or apparent faults are to be directed to

HEAVEN, DEPARTMENT OF FINISHED WORKS

Thank you for your patience.

PART ONE

Dealing With
the Outward Realities

ONE

Change Is Inevitable, Except From a Vending Machine

Sometimes I lie awake at night, and I ask, "Where have I gone wrong?" Then a voice says to me "This is going to take more than one night."

Charlie Brown

Behold, I show you a mystery; we shall not all sleep, but we shall all be changed.

1 Corinthians 15:51

Outside my window, dawn breaks grey over hills muffled in snow. Loath to surrender to the coming day, the frozen night presses its advantage against the glass, frosting the pane as it creeps through. Grateful for the warmth, my hands cradle a cup of hot tea. Closing my eyes, I let the gentle steam from the amber liquid warm my face.

I look out again.

Here and there, poking through melt holes around sleeping trees, bits of grass strain for the coming sun. The melt holes tell me that soon the frigid ground will give way to the life rising from deep within. Soon, in the cycle of all things, spring will end the long night of winter. Soon, men and women thick with wool and flannel will trek through snow-packed woods to gather the sap that even now struggles to rise. Soon, sweet clouds of heady steam will rise from the sugar house across the field.

This is the way of it, I tell myself. No matter how long the winter, no matter how bitter the cold, no matter how frozen the ground, spring always comes, bringing with her the sweetness that has been hidden.

Rise up, my love, my fair one, and come away. For, lo, the winter is past, the rain is over and gone; the flowers appear on the earth; the time of the singing of birds is come, and the voice of the turtle dove is heard in our land; the fig tree putteth forth her green figs, and the vines with the tender grape give a good smell. Arise my love, my fair one, and come away.[1]

Turning from the window, I throw fresh wood on the fire. Pulling the chair over to the hearth, I prop my feet on the hot tiles and rest the mug on my lap. Cooler now, the cup still warms my belly.

Without change, there can be no change, I tell myself. Winter becomes spring because the earth is in a different place in her orbit around the sun. Things change because things change.

Easy enough with the seasons—I don't have to do anything. I can't do anything. I can't make spring come one day earlier than she will. I can't stand like a sentinel between the seasons and stop her from coming, either. Each day will patter past at its petty pace until finally, winter once more creeps into spring.

Not so with the winter in my soul.

There, winter creeps away only as I choose change. I can choose to run to embrace the life struggling to rise from deep within. Or I can choose to stand like a sentinel between the old and the new, forbidding the straining joy to poke through the melt holes around my dreaming heart.

Taking a sip of tea from my rainbow mug, I think about all the changes I've had to make since the day that mug came into my life. Those of you who read *An Affair of the Mind* remember the story. For those of you who didn't, the **Reader's Digest Super-Condensed Version** is that the mug held some flowers my husband, Steve (formerly known as "Jack"*), sent me the morning after I decided to walk out of our then twelve-year marriage. Steve didn't know I was ready to walk out, but God did. That desperate night, God intruded into

---

*If you read *An Affair of the Mind,* you might be wondering who "Steve" is because in that book, my husband's name is "Jack." Steve is my husband's real first name. "Jack and Laurie Hall" were pseudonyms chosen because my publisher required me to write under a pseudonym. However, having a pseudonym began to pose immediate problems for me as I did radio and TV interviews and fulfilled speaking engagements all over the country. Air travel became increasingly burdensome with two names and photo ID for only one of them. In addition, some people were put off by what seemed to them to be a lack of

my hopelessness and told me He would show me how to keep my marriage vows.

The "how" came as God used that rainbow mug to start me on a journey of learning about covenant. You probably know that the rainbow is a symbol of the covenant God made with Noah and every living thing, that He would never again destroy the earth by flood. You might already know about the power of covenant, but back in those days, I knew nothing about it. All I knew was the rainbow was a symbol of the New Age. So, as thrilled as I was that my husband had sent me flowers, I wasn't sure it was OK to keep anything with a rainbow on it because we were sure enough Bible-believing Christians and we had come-out-from-among-them-and-been-separate. (I'm glad God is bigger than our self-righteousness, aren't you?) Anyway, as God assured me that morning so many years ago when I expressed doubt about the propriety of having a rainbow in my home—"I had it first."

As I sat there that long-ago morning, looking at that rainbow and remembering the story about the great Flood, it seemed God was saying to me, "Stormy times are ahead, but I will keep you safe in the ark of my covenant." I didn't tell anyone about this promise; I just cherished it in my heart and pondered it over and over. That day, I started a journey that turned my life upside down. It was kind of like being at the beginning of a treasure hunt and the first clue was "covenant." To find out more about covenant, God drove me into the Word—which I read cover to cover to cover to cover.

"I don't want you to get through the Word, I want the Word to get through you," the Lord seemed to be saying to me. I discovered I had a lot of bad theology—theology which was making it impossible for me to deal effectively with my situation. You can't live beyond what you believe, so God had to dismantle my false beliefs one by one before He could give me a battle plan to begin dealing with what was going on in my marriage.

Over the next fourteen years, God sent me seven rainbows. Three came as mugs, one came as a trivet that said, "Look for the rainbow," two came as real rainbows, and one came as the symbol of the Tres Dias weekend that really

integrity. So, to avoid ongoing hassles, I legally changed my name to Laurie Sharlene Hall (Sharlene being my original first name). Recently, my husband started traveling with me. While there were valid reasons for my publisher's requirement for us to use pseudonyms, many of those issues have been resolved; therefore, we have decided to use my husband's real first name in this book and in all subsequent speaking engagements and joint interviews.

began to open my husband to the healing power of Christ's love.

I never got a rainbow when things were manageable, only when I was truly despairing that God remembered the promise He had given me. Each one came at a turning point, a place where I needed to make a decision. Its arrival was like a special hug from God, almost as if He were telling me, "I haven't forgotten. I am working, even though it's been a long time since there's been outward evidence of My work." And sure enough, shortly after the arrival of each rainbow, a breakthrough in healing would occur.

But I'm getting ahead of myself (or is that behind myself?). Back to the idea of change. I've always known that change is an important part of moving on, and I've always known that somehow I have to choose to change. Figuring out how to act on that knowledge has been the tricky part.

When I first became aware that there were profound problems in my marriage, I tried to do many things to change. I read all the books, attended all the seminars, and did all the Bible studies. And I mean read, attended, and did them. I was the Total Woman. I was the Fascinating Woman. I was the Proverbs 31 Woman. I was the Complete Woman. I was the Excellent Woman. I was the His Needs/Her Neediness Woman. I was the He's From Home Depot, She's From Wal-Mart Woman. I was Some Kind of Woman. It was all *marvelously* effective.

How about you? Are there places deep inside where the joy is struggling to rise? Have you read all the books, attended all the seminars, and done all the Bible studies trying to figure out what's holding that joy back? After giving it your best shot and maybe seeing some small changes in your situation, do you feel like it's really mostly smoke and mirrors? When you listen to the glowing testimonials, do you keep asking yourself, "How come this stuff works for them but I can't quite seem to wrap myself around it enough to have it work for me?" Do you feel like the great cosmic exception to the saving grace of God?

Do you feel like you've been promised the world at the expense of your own soul?

Do you ever think that maybe we've been had? Read on.

TWO

You Can't Get There From Here

Somebody said to me, "But the Beatles were antimaterialistic."
That's a huge myth. John and I literally used to sit down and
say, "Now, let's write a swimming pool."

Paul McCartney

There is a way which seemeth right unto a man, but the ends
thereof are the ways of death.

PROVERBS 14:12

We live in a small rural village in northern Vermont where there are more cows than people. We like it that way.

Our village is the Northeast's premier noncoastal gathering spot for landscape artists. So, you've probably seen our cows, farms, and quiet meadows on a wide variety of paintings, calendars, and postcards. Imagine my surprise one day when I discovered our barn in all its charming decrepitude on a postcard. "Hey, that looks familiar," I said to myself as I pulled the card from the rack. Sure 'nuf, closer inspection revealed the startling truth. We really should mow more often.

Our village is nestled at the base of Mount Mansfield, the highest mountain in a state filled with mountains. The runoff from our mountains feeds a multitude of streams, rivers, and 430 lakes and ponds—more if you count wetlands ponds like the one in the woods below our barn where some industrious beavers have been busily engineering a pretty good lodge and where, one winter, my daughter and I saw a bear's footprints the size of dinner plates when we were cross-country skiing.

Vermont's got so many mountains and so much running water that after fleeing the Nazis, the singing Von Trapp family of *Sound of Music* fame settled a few miles from our village because they said the area reminded them of their native Austria. In Vermont, they could still climb every mountain and ford every stream.

You Can't Get There From Here

Our unique geography has given rise to an old Vermont saying, "You can't get there from here." This means there's often a geographical barrier between where you are and where you want to go. Some of these barriers are seasonal. Take our mountain, for instance. During part of the year, we can drive over it; but from mid-November until late spring, we have to go around it because the state doesn't plow the notch road. Seems they think narrow, snow- and ice-covered roads surrounded on both sides by twenty- to thirty-foot boulders are some kind of hazard for the average driver. During the time the road is closed, what was a ten-mile trip for us stretches to over forty miles as we drive around the mountain.

Other geographical barriers are year-round problems. Running close to 100 miles down the "west coast" of Vermont, Lake Champlain, the largest lake in New England, has only a few bridges and ferry crossings. So those traveling from Vermont to New York have to drive many miles out of their way to find places where they can "cross over."

Yep, it's true. In Vermont, lots of times you can't get there from here.

What Ever Happened to Beaver Cleaver?

Often, in our families we feel like we can't get there from here. We have some idea of how we think our family "ought" to function. For some of us, this idea came from a 1950s television program like "Leave It to Beaver." Ward Cleaver always had the right answers for the Beav (who *never* mouthed off), and June, attired in high heels and freshly starched apron, never failed to dish up a tasty meal from her immaculate kitchen.

Some of us got our ideals from great books like Laura Ingalls Wilder's *Little House on the Prairie* series. According to Laura, whether it was bears, snowy winters, or a bad year for crops, the family pulled together. One for all and all for one. Kids cheerfully helped around the house. Pa (who looked like Michael Landon) was always loyal, faithful, true, and kind to small animals, and Ma never uttered a discouraging word.

Others of us have gone the Christian-family-seminar route. We've attended a variety of workshops or read a number of self-help books designed to explain the biblical view of family life, which as it turns out doesn't look much different than the Cleaver or Ingalls household. The take from most of these books and seminars is if Dad will just assume his place as the head of the household and Mom will just be submissive and all the kids will just remember to respect Mom and Dad, family life will be like the Hallmark card or Taster's Choice ads. Wherever we got our idea of how families "ought" to be, much of the emotional distress we feel in our daily life is directly related to the fact that our family doesn't seem to be able to get there from here.

Moving From the Ideal to the Real

Most of us marched down the aisle with stars in our eyes, thinking we were going to create a wonderful home with our dearly beloved. We thought if we loved enough, tried hard enough, and were sincere enough, somehow the family we were going to create would be like Ward and June Cleaver's or maybe Ma and Pa Ingalls', or at the very least healthy, wealthy, and wise. We didn't expect perfection and we weren't obsessing over making everyone think we somehow had the ideal family. But, we thought, we could be reasonably happy.

Trouble is, for some of us, our home looks more like the Simpsons' than the Ingalls' or the Cleavers'. Move over, Laura and Beaver. Hello, Beavis and Butthead. Others of us have gone past rude, crude, and inexcusable to outright betrayal and maybe even abuse. Still others have reasonably healthy families but, looking at the moral quagmire our society is bogged down in, feel ill-equipped to deal with the reality of behavior choices made by others. "How," they ask themselves, "do we prepare our children to interact with people whose value system is so radically different from ours?"

The Giant Sucking Sound of Today's Moral Vacuum

Make no mistake, this is not your grandfather's generation.

We live in a world where parents lock their seven-year-old daughter in a dog cage.[1] We live in a world where after the jury found the nineteen-year-old defendant "guilty of raping a ten-year-old girl, the judge announced in court that she had cried in her office after hearing the verdict—not because of the heinous crime itself, but because she felt the minimum five-year prison term she had to legally impose was too severe."[2]

We live in a world where one study of 1,700 junior high teens found 65% of boys and 57% of girls believe it's acceptable for a male to force a female to have sex if they've been dating for six months[3] and where the leader of the free world defines whether or not he has had an extramarital affair based on what the definition of the word "is" is.

We live in a world where kids see an average of 10,000 murders on TV by age ten and the average American spends 1,600 hours a year watching television and 300 hours listening to music. The average annual amount of time spent reading books? Only 100 hours.[4]

We live in a country which has "the highest rates of childhood suicide, homicide, and gun-related deaths in the world's 26 richest nations."[5]

We live in a world where, by the year 2000, illegitimate births will surpass divorce as the leading cause of fatherlessness in American homes. In 1960, only 18% of teenagers lived apart from their fathers. That percentage will have risen to 50% by the end of this decade.[6]

How does this lack of emotional support from fathers affect children's behavior? Judith Wallerstein's landmark twenty-five-year study showed that children of divorce are more likely to abuse drugs, become alcoholics, and fear intimacy.

According to other studies comparing children from fatherless homes with children from two-parent homes, children from fatherless homes are:

5 times more likely to commit suicide
32 times more likely to run away
20 times more likely to have behavior disorders
14 times more likely to commit rape (boys)
9 times more likely to drop out of high school
10 times more likely to abuse chemical substances

9 times more likely to end up in a state institution
20 times more likely to end up in prison

The consequences of fatherlessness reach into adulthood. Nashville therapist Tony Rankin says that 95% of all adults in therapy are wrestling with abandonment issues.[7]

Feeling like pulling the blankey over your head and sucking your thumb for a while? Hang on a bit longer, milk and cookies *will* be served.

Turned On, Tuned In, and Dropped on Our Heads

We are a society gagging on the bitter aftertaste of the failed social experiment of the 60s. Do you remember some of the sayings of the 60s?

Turn on, tune in, drop out.
Don't trust anyone over 30.
ALL WE ARE SAYING IS, GIVE PEACE A CHANCE.
HELL NO, WE WON'T GO.
Make Love, Not War.

And the mantra of the decade:

IF IT FEELS GOOD, DO IT.

The 60s generation felt good a lot. We pioneered the sexual revolution. Sex for the sake of sex. Sex without obligation. Sex without commitment. Sex without consequences.

Love, we were told, is free. But free love costs. And it costs big. One of those big costs is the way cohabitation undermines the potential of a couple to make a future marriage work.

"For over 30 years the conventional wisdom has been that, if marriage is relevant at all, living together can let two people know whether they are compatible enough for marriage. It is a concept that increasing numbers of people are buying into. Since 1970, the Census Bureau reports that the number of households made up of unmarried couples has grown eightfold. By the time a woman reaches the age category of 30–34, 49% say they have lived with a man outside marriage.

"But if more and more people are hoping that cohabitation improves their chances of being happily married later, evidence is rapidly mounting that indicates they will be disappointed. Columnist William R. Mattox, Jr., for example, cited recent research that challenges the wisdom of living together. Results include:

- A woman who is living with a man is more than twice as likely to wind up as a victim of domestic violence (Washington State University researcher Jan Stets).
- Women who are cohabiting suffer from depression at rates more than three times that of married women (National Institute of Mental Health).
- Sexual anxiety is more characteristic of this less permanent living arrangement, rather than sexual freedom, and the absence of an enduring commitment tends to actually hinder sexual satisfaction (UCLA researchers Stuart Perlman and Paul Abrahamson).
- Couples who lived together and then married report less satisfaction in their marriage than other couples (National Institute for Healthcare Research).
- Cohabiting couples who then get married have a significantly higher rate of divorce than those who did not live together first (University of Denver researcher Scott Stanley)."[8]

But statistics are a "safe" way to look at what has happened to our society in the wake of the sexual revolution. Take a deep breath and summon up your courage to look behind some of these statistics. And for those of you who are saying, "I don't want to read a whiny book about how we're all going to hell in a handbasket," you need to know that hope is just around the corner, but you've got to know where you are starting from so you can figure out how to get where you want to go.

So, Let Me Put Some Faces on Those Statistics

News report: "Eighteen-year-old Melissa Drexler strangled her newborn son last spring and threw him into the garbage during her senior prom."[9] Zipping up her dress, Melissa leaves the blood-spattered bathroom and returns to the prom to dance the night away.

A young mother who was sexually abused by her stepfather when she was a girl is rejected by her adulterous husband. Her new boyfriend doesn't have time for her two young sons, so she straps them into their carseats and drives the car into a lake, drowning both boys.

The husband of a popular talk show hostess is caught in an adulterous affair by a tabloid. This Christian couple had previously appeared in a marriage video hosted by a best-selling Christian author.

A powerful White House consultant is sacked after his relationship with a high-priced call girl is publicized by a tabloid.

A well-known sportscaster loses his job after charges of gross sexual assault.

A six-year-old girl "beauty queen" is murdered the day after Christmas, her sexually abused body discovered in the basement of her parents' posh home.

The tragic stories go on and on. The bitter harvest of the failed social experiment of free love has come in and we are a society awash with its troubling consequences.

As we near the end of the 20th century, Americans are more concerned about morals now than at any other time in the last sixty years. A poll published in the March 1997 issue of *Emerging Trends* shows that 69% of Americans rate U.S. morals as either somewhat weak or very weak. Only 3% think Americans have strong morals, and 53% are more concerned about our nation's moral problems than they are about our nation's economic problems.[10] Indeed, there are those who argue that many of our economic difficulties can be traced back to moral issues, such as the loss of a biblical work ethic and the breakdown of the nuclear family.

We Might Be Down, but We're Not Out

OK, so everywhere we look, there are signs that the fabric of our society is unraveling. But look again and don't count the family out yet. Despite the current crop of teen movies which show parents as nonessential, according to a survey done by Barna Research Group of Ventura, California, teens want to listen to their parents. When asked to rank those who had "a lot of influence" on their thinking and behavior, teens said:

parents	78%
friends	51%
the Christian faith	48%
the Bible	44%
brothers/sisters	40%
teachers	34%
church pastors/priests	27%
music	25%
television	13%
movies	10%
national political leaders	6%[11]

A recent poll of 272,400 middle school and high school students gave similar results. Respondents ranked parents as the most important influence in their lives and religion as second. However, 36% said they feel that adults don't value what kids think.[12]

Further, for all the handwringing about dysfunctional family-of-origin issues, "current studies negate past theories that children growing up in dysfunctional households would be dysfunctional themselves. In contrast, many abused children are committed to not following in abusive parents' footsteps. For example, studies of poverty-stricken islanders and Cambodian refugees who've settled in Minnesota have resulted in the type of positive conclusions that scientists and others are coming to expect about the popular science of resilience.

"Because of these studies, psychology is no longer focusing on what hurts people but on the resilience that causes them to rise above the hurt. A couple of things are sure. Resilience is attainable for all. However, recovery is long and slow and may not even begin until adulthood.

"Various other observations are being made about those fighting back to lead normal lives:

- The ability to turn around is always there.
- Approximately one-third of all struggling children are showing resilience and doing well in school by adolescence.
- Faith in someone or something is important.
- Family, friends, and coworkers form an encouraging support system.
- Believing in one's own worth and potential is essential."[13]

Forgiveness—the Greatest Resilience Builder Around

The sad statistics in this chapter are almost all a reflection of lives that came unglued when someone broke someone else's heart. "A broken heart who can bear?" the psalmist asks. Understanding the power of forgiveness to heal the brokenhearted and set the captive free is an essential part of shoring up the foundations of a culture gone mad. And all you spiritual warfare buffs take note: forgiveness is the ultimate act of spiritual warfare.

You want to make some demons scream? Try blessing those who curse you, doing good to those who hate you, and praying for those who despitefully use you. You want to bring down spiritual powers in high places? Try forgiving the traumas that allowed those principalities to be set up in the first place. Listen, forgiveness isn't easy and it certainly isn't bloodless, but as you begin to get the hang of it you're going to have more fun than you could possibly imagine.

Forgiveness is the way God calls us back to Himself. Forgiveness is the way we recover that part of ourselves that was ripped off when someone decided to violate our boundaries. Forgiveness is the way we invite our offenders to taste of the goodness of life. Forgiveness is a hand-engraved invitation into the Kingdom of God. In that Kingdom, injustice is dealt with justly, brokenness is dealt with mercifully, and every man occupies his place with a joy unspeakable and full of glory. In that Kingdom, every tear is wiped away and everything that has been lost is found.

Forgiveness is the way we recover our culture.

Thinking It Through

1. What are your concerns about the cultural collapse all around us? How has the prevailing culture made it more difficult for you to parent? to be married? What do you think it would take to protect your family in the midst of the culture wars?

2. From what sources did you develop your ideals about family life? In what ways have you been able to live out those ideals? Which ideals seem beyond your reach? What do you think keeps the ideal from becoming the real?

3. Are there any ways that the fallout from your sexual past is affecting your family life today? Do you think the way we handle our sexuality affects our culture? How?

THREE

I Tried Walking on Water Once and It Didn't Go Well

Without moral ideals a society cannot shape much of a common life. And sometimes one moral ideal—isolated and taken by itself—can undermine all others. For us the language of compassion—perhaps the stench of Christian, or at least Protestant moralism—has done that. Feeling it necessary to affirm every person in whatever state he or she may be, we find it difficult to state and adhere to any standard of conduct. To articulate such an ideal might seem too much like condemning those who do not meet it.[1]

Gilbert Meilander

For they have healed the hurt of the daughter of my people slightly, saying, Peace, peace; when there is no peace.

JEREMIAH 8:11

The son of a well-known atheist becomes a Christian. The woman whose unplanned pregnancy was behind *Roe v. Wade* "gets saved." A well-known television evangelist has an affair and pays to keep the woman quiet; then, he is indicted for bilking ministry investors. While in prison, he experiences a profound sense of the grace of God and comes out a changed man.

Testimonies. We love 'em. We thrill to hear how Christ can change lives. We rejoice when the prodigal comes home. The more time the prodigal spent in the hog pen, and the hoggier that pen was, the more likely we are to make him an icon of the power of forgiveness.

As Christians, we are involved in a faith whose very foundation is based on forgiveness. We believe Christ died on the cross for our sins according to the Scriptures. We believe that when He was dying on that cross, He said, "Father, forgive them for they know not what they do." We believe that He was buried, and that He rose again the third day according to the Scriptures.

Because we believe in Christ's work on the cross, we also believe in personal redemption. We believe that if we confess our sins, He is faithful and just to forgive us our sins and cleanse us from all unrighteousness.[2] We believe that people can be transformed by the renewing of their minds. We believe that old things can pass away and all things can become new. We believe that Christ is able to save us to the uttermost since He is always living to make petition to God and intercede with Him on our behalf.[3]

These beliefs pose some problems for us. *If we don't take in the whole counsel of God about human nature and understand that becoming whole is rarely an overnight phenomenon, these beliefs can make us idealistic about the world.* They can set us up to be taken to the cleaners by someone who has healed only one inch deep. Worse still is the reality that these beliefs, if not taken with the whole counsel of Scripture, can set us up for being fooled by someone who deliberately sets out to deceive us.

The Warm Fuzzies Can Give You a Terrible Rash

A while ago, I received a letter from a woman who had married a man who, while they were dating, confessed that he'd been involved with some homosexuality in his youth. He minimized the involvement and assured her that this was all behind him. Circumstances seemed to vouch for his healing because he was currently a leader in their church. Although all seemed well, just to be sure that she was not fooling herself, she sought her pastor's counsel. "What's past is past," the pastor told her. "Old things are passed away and all things have become new. Isn't Christ wonderful?" So she married this man.

Reality hit her in the face on their wedding night when, in a bride's attempt to seduce her husband, she took off her blouse. Instead of the warm embrace she longed for, he screamed obscenities at her and ran out of the room.

Perhaps, until that very moment, he had been unaware that he was still so sexually broken. But I doubt it. More likely, he had his own doubts about his ability to relate sexually to a woman.

The cynic would say this man married knowing good and well that he wasn't ready for a heterosexual relationship and may even have been planning to use marriage as a smokescreen so that others would have no clue that he was still struggling with homosexual desires. The kinder and gentler among us would say this man was hoping against hope that marriage would somehow cure him, idealistically believing that if he just showed up at the altar, God would somehow take care of the honeymoon.

Whichever view is correct, at the heart of this situation is both an appalling lack of integrity and an appalling naiveté. The husband, whether through intentional deceit or self-deception, withheld vital information that would have helped this woman make a better decision for her life. The woman and her pastor, who had very limited understandings of the difficulty of healing the sexually broken, lived in a fantasy world where compassion overruled common sense. This leads us to a second problem our belief in redemption causes us—*we tend to confuse forgiveness with compassion.*

Forgiveness Is Not Airbrushing Reality

Gilbert Meilander says, "Compassion, taken alone and severed from deeper, richer understandings of our nature and destiny, kills morality. Taken as the sole moral principle it undercuts our ability to articulate an ideal for human life."[4] I would add that, taken alone, compassion devastates our ability to truly forgive those who have hurt us because compassion can make us reluctant to confront evil—and *confronting evil is an essential element of forgiveness.*

Taken alone, compassion can also set us up to be manipulated by someone who hasn't really repented, who is only sorry to be forced to deal with the shame and inconvenience of having been caught.

Forgiveness never airbrushes reality. It looks the behavior full in the face and asks, "What response to this behavior is just, what response is merciful, and what response keeps me in proper relationship with God?"[5] Sometimes the answer to that question involves setting some pretty strong boundaries where very little trust is extended, encouraging loved ones to honestly acknowledge what they've done. That can make us compassionate types uncomfortable. But sometimes it's the only way the behavioral changes necessary for a relationship to be restored will occur.

This is how God operates. He allows us to face our consequences so we will grow up and make better choices the next time. Why? Because consequences are a reflection of our choices, and our choices are a reflection of the image we hold of ourselves. God invites us to remember that we are created in His image and His likeness. He calls us back to who we are. He says, "Have you completely forgotten the divine word of appeal and encouragement in which you are reasoned with and addressed as sons?"[6] Like the father of the prodigal, He weeps while we fill our bellies full of hog slop. He allows us to gag on the garbage. Then, when we finally come to ourselves and realize we are sons of the Most High God, not pigs, He rejoices and welcomes us home with open arms.

Oh Goody, I Get to Forgive

When I realized that this book needed to be about forgiveness, I approached the project with a degree of enthusiasm usually reserved for a root canal. "What can I *honestly* say about forgiveness?" I asked myself. I still had a lot of forgiveness issues to work through about what had happened in my marriage. What does forgiveness look like when your husband has presented himself to you and to your church community as a model Christian man for the first twenty-one years of your marriage, all the while living a double life filled with pornography, strip shows, and prostitutes?

When I say my husband Steve led a double life, I don't mean that I overlooked the obvious. I asked questions about his long work hours. I kept asking him what was causing the drastic personality changes I was observing. I knew something was wrong, but I had no way of knowing about the private hellhole pornography had led him into—only one time in twenty-seven years of marriage had I seen pornography in our home.

I never would have guessed my husband was involved in deliberate deception and sexual perversion. When I met him, he had all the right credentials. Steve grew up on the mission field. He was working at the White House in the days before Watergate, in the days before Zippergate. In those days most of us thought having a White House security clearance meant something about your character. After all, in order to get one, you have to pass the FBI's thorough background check. They go to every place you've ever lived and talk to practically everyone who's ever known you. Knowing that Steve had passed that kind of inspection helped to vouch for his character.

The deception was deepened when, after we left Washington, my husband spent seven years on the staff of a large church in the South. During that time his personality changes became much more marked. But he justified abandoning me physically and emotionally, claiming he needed time to serve the Lord.

Those of you who read my book, *An Affair of the Mind,* are familiar with our story. In *An Affair of the Mind,* you learned how pornography implodes the soul through fantasy. You came to understand the incredible selfishness that drives lust and the devastation it brings to families. Lust objectifies all others and demands that they fill up its bottomless pit of need. Thus, one destroyed soul can destroy a marriage and a family. You also learned there is hope. You know how God sovereignly revealed the truth about my husband and how I began the arduous journey back to wholeness.

Fifteen years down the road from the moment God apprehended me, the night I was ready to walk out on my marriage, I find myself still asking the questions, "What does it mean to forgive when the person you married has committed fraud against you by intentionally misrepresenting who he or she is and then, when the truth comes out, tries to make it look like the problem was all your fault? What does it mean to forgive when there are ongoing consequences for wrong behavior choices? What does it mean to forgive when the character issues that led someone to think he or she could treat you with such total disdain are still unresolved? What does it mean to forgive when your children have irrevocably lost their childhood to this kind of devastation? How do I forgive myself for the times I abandoned them in the midst of the craziness? What does it mean to forgive when there are rifts in the parent-child relationship that just rip what's left of your heart right to shreds? Finally, how do I forgive others for judging me?"

After publication of *An Affair of the Mind,* I received many hundreds of letters from readers whose lives had been irrevocably changed by evil. They were asking similar questions.

- What does forgiveness look like in my situation?
- How can I forgive without opening myself up to further abuse?
- How can I forgive without losing myself in the process?
- Is there any hope for my family?

I also have received many letters from desperate men whose wives had decided to either separate from them or divorce them. These men wanted me to speak with their wives and assure them that things would work out, that they could now trust their husbands to live honorably ... that fairy tales would come true (it could happen to you).

I Learned About Forgiveness on My Face

I've had a lot of opportunities to learn about forgiveness. As I was trying to work through forgiving my husband, someone I dearly loved, deeply respected, and profoundly trusted stunned me with great evil. I was completely unaware that such pain was possible. For an entire year, I daily cried rivers of groanings from broken places too deep for utterance.

With all this experience, you'd think by now I'd be a good forgiver. But the truth is, I still struggle to know what it means to forgive. I would like you to think that I've always kept my cool under fire. But the truth is, I've had times when my anger over betrayal has turned me into a wild and howling woman.

I would like to tell you that I have always been the person I want to be. But, sadly, the truth is that sometimes, the pain and confusion have been so great that I've lost myself in the midst of it all. I would like to report that I have always known the right thing to do in a crunch and that I've done that right thing cheerfully and well. Here we go again. The real truth is this: sometimes I haven't had a clue what the right thing is. And sometimes I've known what the right thing is and I've refused to do it. I've sat there like a spoiled brat and said, "You can't make me."

I'd like to be able to say that I've always felt only love for those who've hurt me. Bend down so I can whisper this one in your ear. *Sometimes, my heart has screamed for murder.*

This book is not about a forgiveness that reeks with piety. I tried walking on water once and it didn't go well.

Forgiveness Is Not for Weenies

The only authority I have for speaking to you about the subject of forgiveness is the authority of truth. I won't try to take you someplace where I haven't been and I won't tell you that the journey we're going to take together will be easy. Weenies need not apply.

The journey to forgiveness is not along a broad and easy path. It's a hard, narrow way that's compacted by pressure. It's the road less traveled. However, should you decide to take it, you'll find the views along the way make it worth the effort.

Part of the struggle is trying to understand our model for forgiveness in motion—Jesus Christ. Often we think of the cross as the defining moment of forgiveness, but everything Jesus did from the time He hit planet Earth was an act of forgiveness. This includes the seemingly opposite extremes of gently pardoning an adulteress[7] while bitingly condemning religious hypocrites,[8] as well as tenderly holding and blessing the children one moment, then driving money changers out of the temple with a whip the next.[9] Jesus fit no molds. He broke them, and in breaking them, He drove the hyper-religious people of His day nuts.

The moral of the story is that the way we "walk out" forgiveness may not make any sense to those observing, especially the hyper-religious who seek safety in lives sterilized of their humanity. Fearful of being either hot or cold, the Scribes and Pharisees among us and within us are much more comfortable with a surface piety that never does battle with strong emotions, doubt, despair, or risk-taking. Such lukewarmness not only renders our lives dry and barren wastelands devoid of spontaneity and joy, it also puts stumbling blocks in the path of true reconciliation with those who have offended us.

Forgiveness Is a Mystery

Jesus said, "Greater love hath no man than this, that a man lay down his life for his friends." Then, Jesus defined what He meant by friends: "You are my friends if you do whatsoever I command you."[10] In other words, there was a qualifier here. In order to be a friend of Jesus, you needed to keep His commandments. Liking Him didn't count. Wandering around after Him in the desert didn't count. Saying He was the Son of God didn't count. You had to put your money where your mouth was and actually obey Him to be considered His friend. You had to stop singing, "I Did It My Way," and start singing, "I Surrender All." You had to give up your own agenda and abandon yourself to His plan and purpose.

Jesus' statement made His disciples think about their commitment to each other and to Him. He challenged those who were continually jockeying for the position of "greatest in the Kingdom" to evaluate whether they loved in the greatest way a man can. Then, while they were still reeling from their inability to find it in their hearts to be truly great, Jesus confounded them all by going beyond the greatest kind of love that a man can have. Jesus laid down His life, not for His friends, but for His enemies.[11]

Man, that's *radical* forgiveness. Radical forgiveness is a mystery. Radical forgiveness goes far beyond extending grace to a friend who is having a bad hair day. Radical forgiveness goes far beyond finding compassion for the brokenness behind a spouse's betrayal. Radical forgiveness goes far beyond understanding why a stranger mistreated you.

I'm not saying that walking a mile in another's shoes isn't a great perspective changer. It is. Empathy is one of the ways we develop brotherly love. Trying on the other guy's moccasins teaches us the compassion that lets us find it in our hearts to release resentment. Understanding, empathy, and compassion are wonderful character qualities, and we all need to develop them. But may I gently suggest that we don't absolutely have to be followers of Jesus to show our offenders understanding, empathy, or compassion. People of many different religious persuasions are capable of cultivating these graces, and there are some good books out there that can help you learn how to do just that.

The Place of Desperate Dependence

Friends, this book isn't about empathetic forgiveness in which you come to understand that the person who hurt you is really "just a friend you haven't met yet." This book is about forgiving when you can't understand no matter how hard you try. This book is about forgiving when your soul has been bent, folded, spindled, and otherwise mutilated by someone who refused to regard you as a person worthy of being treated with dignity and respect. This book is about falling on the cross and dying to phony ways of dealing with sin. This book is about being holy people in an unholy world. This book is about *radical* forgiveness.

This book is about desperate dependence on Jesus.

Thinking It Through

1. In what ways have you confused forgiveness with compassion? How has that confusion kept you from confronting evil?

2. Have you ever airbrushed reality? What happened as a result?

3. What are your basic questions about how forgiveness works? How do consequences for the offender help forgiveness work better?

4. Is there an offense you can't find it in your heart to forgive? How is that offense poisoning your soul?

FOUR

The Emperor Has No Clothes

When we can not ward off the truth with any other pretext, we flee from it by ascribing it to a fierce temper, impatience and immodesty.[1]

Martin Luther

What shall we say then? Shall we continue in sin, that grace may abound? God forbid. How shall we, that are dead to sin, live any longer therein?

ROMANS 6:1-2

(Author's note: Promise Keepers is a wonderful organization. I remember when I first heard about it, I felt it was part of what God says He is going to do in Malachi 4—turn the hearts of fathers back to their children. The more I learned about PK, the more I loved it. I even dedicated my book, An Affair of the Mind, *to Promise Keepers. Coach McCartney and his team are godly men who are dedicated to the task to which God has called them. The story below is not a commentary on PK. Rather, it is about a situation which tellingly portrays how poorly we as a church are doing in engaging our culture.)*

The article said the local chapter of the National Organization for Women was hosting an informational meeting to discuss the reasons why NOW had declared war on Promise Keepers. The evening would feature a documentary that would reveal the subversiveness of this relic of patriarchy as well as including time for discussion about What Could Be Done. My group of local PKers decided to attend.

39

The big night arrived. As we entered the meeting room, we were handed sheets of paper "proving" how Promise Keepers, Focus on the Family, and just about every other well-known Christian organization were somehow collaborating in a vast "right-wing conspiracy" to relegate women to the barefoot and pregnant status of yesteryear. Then the lights were dimmed, and on the screen in front of us appeared clip after grainy clip of Bill McCartney talking about "the blood," as if Coach were proclaiming *jihad* on women rather than talking about the precious blood of Christ. The *coup de grace*, the evidence that was supposed to overwhelmingly convince the audience that the Promise Keepers movement was dangerous, was clips from something called "Promise Reapers" seminars where, according to the video, women learned they just need to be mind-numbed, "submissive" robots. Throughout the room, there were audible sounds of steam rising from ears attached to soon-to-be-talking heads.

As soon as the lights came up, several men vigorously defended Coach, asserting that any woman would willingly submit herself to a godly man and that PK was trying to teach men how to be godly. Several wives spoke of their gratitude to PK for helping their husbands become better men.

Then a woman stood up and said her ex-husband was a pastor who had physically abused her. After years of struggling to figure out how to protect herself while obeying the "submission teaching," she had finally divorced her husband, who had received great sympathy from his church for having such a rebellious wife. She was adamant that she didn't want *anything* to do with Christianity.

Next, a man who was in charge of a weekly group therapy session for batterers asked the Promise Keepers to help him understand how the teachings of Promise Keepers were different than the mindset of the batterer who believes that women must be kept in subjection. Finally, a woman from the Women's Rape Crisis Center and a woman from the local battered women's shelter stood up and asked similar questions. They said they would like to open up a dialogue to help them understand where the church and Promise Keepers were coming from and how they might work with them in the future. They were hoping this could be the first of many discussions that would shed light on the church's stand on these issues.

Several Promise Keepers stood and repeated over and over that PK teaches men how to be godly and that any woman would want to submit to a godly man. One of the men repeatedly shook his finger as he emphasized his points.

The therapist then asked these men to explain what they did to help those in their small groups who might have a problem with anger. "What does accountability mean?" the therapist wanted to know. "Do you check to see if what the men are telling you is true?" Again came the rote answer that PK teaches men to be godly, which is what women really want.

As the evening wound down, there was no further mention of ongoing discussions. The blatant slant of the NOW "documentary" had confirmed the worst stereotypes the Promise Keepers held of the feminists, and the inability of the Promise Keepers to answer the real questions and concerns of the feminists had played to NOW's worst stereotypes of conservative Christian males. Missed opportunities like this are why the church is increasingly considered irrelevant to society.

Do I duck now, or will you hold the rocks a while longer?

A Flickering Light Set on a Shrinking Hill

Despite our increasing reliance on science and technology, Americans want to believe in something bigger than and better than ourselves. Ninety-five percent of Americans claim to believe in God.[2] Not only do we believe in God, we want to talk about Him and hear about what He's doing in the world today. "According to a poll reported in *TV Guide,* 61% of television watchers would like to see more references to God, church and spiritual activities, and 82% would approve of more discussion of moral issues."[3]

Most of those who believe in God consider themselves Christians. With 262 million adherents, Christianity is the largest religion in North America. Sounds pretty good until you realize the church's .8% annual growth rate falls behind both America's .9% population growth rate and the growth rates of most of the other major religions in North America. Hinduism is growing at an annual rate of 3.38%. Buddhism lags a bit behind with an annual growth rate of 2.75%.[4] Even nonreligious people and atheists, with group growth rates of 1.1% and 2% respectively, are recruiting more folks than the local church if you look at growth on a percentage basis.[5]

Further, while it is encouraging that "adult Sunday school attendance has grown for the first time in this decade and the number of adults saying they are born-again Christians rose from 36% in 1994 to 43% in 1997, church attendance by those 70 and older has been declining more substantially than expected and the number of unchurched adults has not decreased."[6] Finally, according to the Barna Report, "Christians' commitment to the faith is very superficial with only one in three born-again Christians claiming to be absolutely committed."[7]

Historically, it has been the church's job to teach morals by defining right and wrong. Yet a poll conducted by George Barna reveals that only 47% of Christian men believe there are moral truths that are unchanging.[8] Among those claiming to be born-again, Barna found that only half read Scripture during the week[9] and only 35% are likely to rely upon Scripture for answers when they need to make moral or ethical decisions.[10]

The refusal to acknowledge that there is a higher authority than our own intellect or perceived needs affects how we handle our sexuality. According to *Sex in America: A Definitive Survey*, only 50.5% of conservative Protestants say that religious belief always guides their sexual behavior and that premarital, extramarital, and homosexual sex is wrong. Among mainline Protestants, 30.9% had a traditional view of sex; among Catholics, only 22%.

Sex in America also found that 41% of all men and 16% of all women (including conservative Protestants) reported having done one of the following in the previous twelve months:

- watching an X-rated movie
- visiting a club with semi-nude or nude dancers
- purchasing sexually explicit books, magazines, erotic devices, or sex toys
- calling a sex phone number[11]

According to a 1996 survey of men who attended Promise Keepers stadium events, better than 50% of them had employed pornography within one week prior to attending that event, indicating a level of pornography usage that's 10% higher than that of the general population. Bringing the focus in a bit more sharply, another study found that 51% of the married Christian men it surveyed were masturbating to pornography. This means that on any given Sunday morning, as many as half the marriages in the congregation are suffering from the devastating effects of this hidden enemy of marriage.

Paralyzed Pastors Preaching From Powerless Pulpits

The very nature of the pastorate makes those occupying that position vulnerable to personal and family difficulties. No matter how complex the situation, pastors are expected to know what to say and how to say it, and they are expected to keep saying it long after everyone else has given up and gone home. Pastors are expected to take personal criticism with an unnatural degree of grace and confront gently when they discover people gossiping viciously behind their backs. They are expected to be available 24 and 7, often at mealtimes and frequently late at night.

Pastors routinely battle "sheep bite," creatively navigate their way through church squabbles, preach the word in season and out of season, and live in glass houses while those looking in often throw stones. They are expected to do all this on the basis of a seminary education that stresses intellectual knowledge of the Bible and expository preaching techniques, with much less time spent in learning how to resolve conflict with parishioners and maintain personal wholeness. Combine the unique pressures of the ministry with the fact that pastors have large amounts of unaccounted-for time, close contact with females in crisis, as well as possible unhealed personal baggage, and you have a setup for sexual brokenness.[12]

Recently, a school which for many years has been one of the premier training grounds for evangelical pastors and missionaries called and asked me to come speak to their student body about pornography. They were concerned about the amount and type of pornography left in the school Dumpsters after their annual pastors' conferences.

Everywhere I go, I hear of pastors involved in homosexuality, heterosexual immorality, and pornography. I'm in contact with pastors from all over the world who have struggled with or are struggling with sexual brokenness. Laurie, you may say, this is the "blue Volkswagen syndrome" (you know, you buy a blue Volkswagen and suddenly you see them everywhere).

Perhaps, but consider further. Sexual addiction is the number one reason Christians come to one major counseling center in Chicago. The greater percentage of the men coming for counsel are lay workers or pastoral staff of evangelical churches. H.B. London, Director of Pastoral Counseling for Focus on the Family, reports that the number of pastors calling Focus' toll-free pastoral counseling center for help with pornography tripled in 1998.[13]

Further, I have in my files many letters from wives of pastors, elders, deacons, worship leaders, missionaries, and youth leaders who read *An Affair of the Mind* and then wrote to tell me their stories of how their husbands had betrayed both their ordination vows and their marriage vows.

I regularly come into contact with those who minister to pastors. Time after time, I hear their estimates about the percentages of pastors they deal with who are struggling with pornography and sexual brokenness issues. The numbers are similar no matter whom I talk with or where he or she is from. Because this percentage comes from personal observations and not a study that relies on scientific polling techniques, I won't record it in this book, but I can tell you it's *very* high—higher than the percentage of men in the pews who struggle.

The Emperor Has No Clothes

In addition to having trouble living out a biblical sexual morality, the church also struggles with the specter of domestic violence. Some "estimates conclude that 25% of women in the church are either enduring or are survivors of domestic abuse. Small wonder, then, that many feminist groups have attacked Christian organizations (such as Promise Keepers) that encourage men to return to biblical principles of family leadership. Their complaints are bolstered when wives in abusive situations are advised by pastors to return and subject themselves to their husbands. Too often, ... abused wives are enjoined to try harder, pray harder, 'as if the abuse were something the victim deserved or could control.'"[14]

Maybe these statistics point to why the church doesn't do so well when it comes to keeping her families together. While "23% of the general population divorce, people who consider themselves evangelical have a slightly higher divorce rate (27%). Those who consider themselves to be fundamentalists have an even higher rate (30%). Of evangelicals who divorced, 87% did so after accepting Christ, even though it can be presumed they knew of the Scriptures which discourage it."[15]

No wonder the church, frequently more interested in controlling (or condoning) behavior than restoring the soul, often either stands by helplessly wringing her hands with a plea for compassion for those engaging in gross sin or else issues meaningless platitudes that offer the broken little hope that the future will be any different than the past.

The emperor has no clothes and everybody knows it but us.

THE READER: "Stop! Stop! I've got a question."

LAURIE: "Hey, you can't do that!"

THE READER: "I've ploughed through plenty of your thoughts; now I've got a few thoughts of my own. I'd like to enter into dialogue. You know, chitchat back and forth about some of the stuff you're saying."

LAURIE: "Go for it."

THE READER: "OK! There's some pretty grim stuff in here about the state of the church. Are you saying we've really missed the mark on what it means to live in a world filled with sinners?"

LAURIE: "Uh huh. We have a theology that says all have sinned and come short of the glory of God, but then we gloss over that reality."

THE READER: "Yeah, I've noticed that. We expect that everyone in the church is your ordinary garden variety sinner who really wants to do what's right, but every now and then has a bad hair day or is just plain dumb about human relations. It's as if all the church needs to do is give the ordinary sinner some tips on communication and bring him up to speed on what other people's needs are and, for the most part, he's good to go."

LAURIE: "Exactly."

THE READER: "But not everyone is an ordinary sinner. There are also people out there who just don't get it."

LAURIE: "You've noticed that, too?"

THE READER: "Yep. I have a friend who's married to a guy who drinks too much. He comes home and wrecks the joint and smacks the kids around. She's afraid he's going to hurt them badly sometime, or maybe even kill someone when he climbs behind the wheel. But the morning after the binge, he cries and says he's going to get it together. He promises he'll never drink again and begs her for another chance. Her pastor says the tears show her husband's repented and she's got to believe the best of him. But I notice that it doesn't take long before the guy's back at the bottle."

LAURIE: "So, you're saying the 'usual approach' disempowers one spouse and enables the other spouse to remain a fool."

THE READER: "You've got it. Something else troubles me. I've noticed there are some people out there who are quietly calculating about how they dismantle others. They work really hard to make you think they're great people while secretly trying to figure out how to take you to the cleaners. I don't think I've ever heard any sermons on how to deal with situations like that."

LAURIE: "I've noticed that, too. The church often operates as if everyone's playing by the rules, as in, 'If I ask you to stop doing something that's hurting me—politely enough—you'll say, "Oh, I'm so sorry, I didn't realize I was being such a jerk," and stop immediately.'"

THE READER: "The maxim seems to be, 'Whatsoever thou doest, doeth it nicely and everything will turn out OK.'"

LAURIE: "Uh huh. What we really need to know is what it means to live and love in a fallen world."

THE READER: "Sounds like you're talking about learning how to forgive."

LAURIE: "Keep turning the pages."

Thinking It Through

1. How might you engage in discussions with those who have genuine questions about the discrepancy between what the church says she stands for and the way Christians sometimes behave? What would help you be more effective in these encounters?

2. What are some ways we are not telling ourselves the truth about the way sexual sin is devastating Christians? How does your church handle those who ask for help with their sexual struggles? Is this approach bringing lasting healing to people?

3. In what ways are you more interested in controlling behavior than in restoring the soul? What platitudes have you given (or received) about how easy it is to "fix" bad behavior?

FIVE

When the Prince You're Kissing Turns Into a Frog

Love is an ideal thing, marriage is a real thing; a confusion
of the ideal with the real never goes unpunished.

Goethe

And this you do with double guilt; you cover the altar of the
Lord with tears shed by your unoffending wives, divorced
by you that you might take heathen wives, and with your
own weeping and crying out because the Lord does not
regard your offering any more or accept it with favor at
your hand. Yet you ask, "Why does He reject it?" Because
the Lord was witness to the covenant made at your marriage between you and the wife of your youth, against
whom you have dealt treacherously and to whom you were
faithless. Yet she is your companion and the wife of your
covenant.

MALACHI 2:13, 14, AMPLIFIED

Dear Laurie,

I'm still grieving the loss of my young womanhood and the countless
nights I went to bed frustrated sexually and wounded in the heart. It is hard
to look at my face in mid-life and wonder how my husband rejected me when
I was at my best—I was really pretty.

I constantly wonder what I could've done differently. The question absolutely
hounds me! I went through the stages you did of being obedient, submitting

even over tiny issues while straining at cows, and ministering to his needs and enjoying it, even when mine were missed. All the while, I suffered terrible guilt from the increasing breakdowns I was having due to exhaustion.

I just realized today that for years I have been afraid to go to bed before my husband. I was afraid that in meeting my needs for rest I would somehow be neglecting his sexual or emotional needs. Actually, I did try, simply saying, "I'm tired." But he felt rejected and it took days and days to build him up again. In the process, I was punished by his lack of involvement in the home and children's lives (as little as it was).

Worse, he would spend days picking at me until I exploded. I wanted so much to have an emotional connection with him that I was willing to do it through anger if that was the only way he would hear me. I still suffer from sleeplessness and the inability to say, "Good night."

I am held hostage by his quickness to give up. Why do I feel I must bolster him? I suddenly realized his passivity is a character choice, a sinful choice that has nothing to do with me, though I've been blamed often for it. By default the Christian community assumes the wounded must be under some sort of judgment or discipline from the Lord. It is almost a Hindu approach to life— fatalistic, instead of a good clean anger after a wrong done.

I don't think I could have done anything else in my situation except pray more for truth. I was living within the context of a lie. I wasn't responsible for that lie. The false data that came in gave me wrong clues as well as wrong ideas about myself, the Lord, and my husband. I stood up many, many times for what was right and received cursing for it, and my husband's further withdrawal. And I was already starving from the lack of connection.

I remember once my husband shoved me, tore keys out of my hand, and swore at me when I ran out of a Bible Time he was having because I was upset that he was demeaning me. I was afraid to tell him how I felt because I thought that would be unsubmissive since a good wife should like everything her husband says and does and not suggest any changes. Afterward, I ran to all of his counseling books—not one of the Christian ones dealt with male physical abuse. I had to go to a secular book at the library to find any information on abuse. In fact, not a single Christian source I checked told me that these "minor" abuses not only weren't minor but were contrary to God. I was so afraid of being viewed as "the problem," when really I had fallen apart in anger because I was overly exhausted. He really knew how to paint me bad.

I once thought I would love to write a book called *Guerrilla Submission, i.e., How to Submit When It Isn't Nice Out There.* There needs to be a lot more dialogue to understand how to submit within an evil situation.

Signed,
Hurting

Are you as moved by that letter as I am? It came from a woman who had eschewed the feminist philosophy of self-fulfillment. Instead, she put all her eggs in the basket of the traditional family. Diligently following all the rules she was told would create a godly family, she "came home" to give herself to her husband and children. From all appearances, this family had it all together.

Highly respected by both their church and their community, this family was willing to allow God to plan the size of their family (they refused to use birth control because the books they had read about creating a godly family said that using birth control was a selfish attempt to avoid a blessing God wants to send you). This family was willing to birth their children at home. This family was willing to take on the incredible responsibility of homeschooling their many children. This family was willing to exhaust itself swimming against the tide of a culture that is anti-family.

This family was rotting from the inside out.

The husband, who had diligently investigated the concept of patriarchy, was trying to live up to an incredible standard of what it means to be a godly man—all the while hiding a secret life that involved sexual perversion. His private hell and the guilt accompanying it were hidden by mind games that he played on his wife. The charade almost killed both of them.

THE READER: "I can't stand this. What hope do any of us have if these people who tried so hard couldn't make it work? What went wrong here, anyway?"

LAURIE: "The basic problem? They were conforming themselves to roles and rules rather than character and covenant."

THE READER: "I'm getting a little uneasy here. Are you saying roles and rules aren't important?"

LAURIE: "I'm saying whatever the roles are, whatever the rules are, God does not intend for those roles and rules to include fraud and abuse."

THE READER: "Fraud and abuse. That's pretty strong language."

LAURIE: "Yes. But it reflects the reality of what was going on here, where people were going through the motions in kind of a shadow world, never touching the true reality of their lives."

THE READER: "OK, so the husband's deceit was a type of fraud. He pretended to be someone he wasn't—pretty devastating, especially when he was pretending to be someone so wonderful. But it seems to me there was another type of fraud going on here. These people had been sold a fantasy. Is that part of the fraud—the belief that roles and rules can create a relationship, as if you could build a home by following a formula?"

LAURIE: "Exactly. You can create a structure following a formula, but you can't create intimacy."

THE READER: "I think I'm catching on. The roles and rules are the starting point but only because they show us our poverty. They show us that even when you give it your best shot, something is still missing."

LAURIE: "Right. The roles and rules define where we fail, but they don't give us the power to succeed. They show us the outward form but give us no inner power to assume that shape. And all the while they condemn us for falling short."

THE READER: "Reminds me of what Paul said about the law—it's important because it points the way, but it gives us no wings to fly there. It commands us to bring forth life, but it has no life-giving force within it. Instead, as Paul says, 'And the commandment, which was ordained to life, I found to be unto death.'[1] Could this be part of the reason why people who are trying so hard to have godly homes by following roles and rules are failing?"

Let Me Marinate on That for a While

When Servant first asked me to write a book on spiritual warfare for the family, I was temporarily stumped. There are many good books and a number of seminars out there that focus on the family. Some of the books and seminars focus on the roles men and women are expected to occupy in the traditional family. The rules for staying in those roles are carefully detailed. Other books and seminars equip the couple to develop good communication skills. The main presupposition of most of these marriage-equipping resources seems to be that if people know their roles and can talk to each other, the majority of marriage problems can be solved.

There are also many good books out there on spiritual warfare. They tell you how to pray against and how to pray for, how to cast out demons, and how to recognize strongholds. What, I wondered, could I possibly add to the discussion? So, I "marinated" on the idea for almost a year before I knew how to tackle the subject. Letters like the one at the beginning of this chapter, and hundreds more just like it, helped move me along.

Those of you who read *An Affair of the Mind* know that when this adventure started I played by the rules and understood the roles. You also know I lacked a theological framework for the concept of spiritual warfare. In the last fifteen years, I've been on a steep learning curve. In a nutshell, here's what I've learned about spiritual warfare:

> *Spiritual warfare is the process of*
> *replacing lies with truth.*

Satan is the father of lies, so some limit spiritual warfare to battling demons. I'm not sure this is the best approach. Don't get me wrong. I believe there could be some demons involved. Steve and I have been through deliverance ministry, and it was a really important part of the healing process. But I've noticed that we're fully capable of deceiving ourselves, apart from any outside help.

Usually, when we fall for a lie, we don't think it's a lie. We believe it because we think it's the truth. Or maybe we think it's better than the truth we don't want to believe. However, our failure to recognize that a false belief is a lie doesn't deliver us from the consequences that come when we act on that lie. "There is a way which seemeth right unto a man, but the end thereof are the ways of death."[2]

In addition to faking ourselves out, I've also noticed that we're fully capable of being completely aware that we're about to practice evil and choosing to do it anyway. We lie to ourselves that we can have our cake and eat it, too. Self-deception and selfishness come from the human heart, and while it would be tempting to blame it all on the devil, friends, the plain truth is the heart is "deceitful above all things, and desperately wicked."[3]

Chapter one of Paul's Letter to the Romans, which is kind of the signature passage for the Last Days' Little Shop of Horrors, details a whole shopping list of really bad things we're going to be involved in as this age winds down— slander, envy, murder, jealousy, faithlessness, heartlessness, treachery, deceit, and cruelty—and that's just for starters. Notice there isn't a single demon mentioned in the whole list. Instead, responsibility for the mess we find our- selves in is laid at the doorstep of Free Will. I encourage you to read the whole passage and notice the following verses (italics and brackets are mine):

> In verse 19: For that which is known about God is *evident to them and made plain in their inner consciousness,* because God Himself has shown it to them.

> In verse 20: For ever since the creation of the world His invisible nature and attributes, that is, His eternal power and divinity, have been made intel- ligible and clearly discernible in and through the things that have been made—His handiworks. So *men are without excuse altogether without any defense or justification.*

> In verse 25: Because *they exchanged* the truth of God for a lie and *worshiped* and served the creature rather than the Creator, Who is blessed forever!

> In verses 28-29a: And so, since *they did not see fit* to acknowledge God or approve of Him or consider Him worth the knowing, God gave them over to a base and condemned mind to do things not proper or decent but loathsome, Until they were filled ... [with all the things they had practiced].

> In verse 32: Though *they are fully aware* of God's righteous decree that those who do such things deserve to die, *they not only do them themselves but approve and applaud others who practice them.*[4]

As you read through this passage, it becomes chillingly apparent that it is because of repeated, deliberate bad choices that "God gave them over." It's not stated that He gave them over to demons; it seems that He gave them over to themselves. I'm not sure which is worse.

Those of you who bought this book so you could learn how to engage in "power encounters" to break bondages in your families need to know that the first power encounter we all need to have is a power encounter with truth.

The truth is what sets us free. And the truth is, we give the enemy legal ground to come and harass us. If you don't deal with the legal ground, deliverance is a disaster waiting to boomerang on you. The evil spirit may leave, but if you don't take care of the lies that allowed him to take up residence in the first place, he will come back, bringing his buddies with him, and you'll be worse off than you were before.

By way of illustration, not long ago I spoke with a man who had been through deliverance for voyeurism. He would peek in his neighbors' windows, watching them undress. After a brush with the law, he went for deliverance. During the deliverance, he had a physical sensation where he literally felt something come off him. For the next year, he was clean. He didn't peep. Then one day, he was walking down the road and came across a pornographic magazine. Automatic pilot took over. The next thing he knew, he had another arrest on his record.

What happened? He had never dealt with the legal ground. He didn't examine the belief system that led him into trouble in the first place. He didn't understand the concept of free will. The consequences were devastating for everyone involved.

The Wheel Is Turning, but the Hamster Is Dead

Jesus said the truth will make you free.[5] But, all too often, the "truths" we believe lead us into bondage. When the mess we're in is getting worse, we try harder to apply the same "truth." Then, when the inevitable failure comes, we think it's because we need to try harder still. Rarely does it occur to us to ask ourselves if our failure to find freedom comes not from lack of trying but from lack of truth.

The brutal reality is this: If the truth will make us free and we aren't free, we aren't telling ourselves the truth. The wheel is turning, but the hamster is dead.

For some, the hamster dies because we are lying to ourselves about our personal character flaws. For others, the hamster takes it heavy because our sense of what we need to be doing and where we need to be going and how we can get there is *way* off. In other words, we are lost in our trespasses and sins. And sometimes, in the midst of our lostness, we think the devil is out to get us when, in reality, the consequences we are experiencing come from the very hand of God as He tries to knock some sense into our heads.

While it is sometimes true that the way to solve our problems is to come up with better answers, it is more often true that the solution lies in asking better questions. Perhaps this is one reason why James says, "Consider it wholly joyful, my brethren, whenever you are enveloped in or encounter trials of any sort or fall into various temptations. Be assured and understand that the trial and proving of your faith bring out endurance and steadfastness and patience. But let endurance and steadfastness and patience have full play and do a thorough work, so that you may be people perfectly and fully developed with no defects, lacking in nothing."[6]

Peter agrees. "You should be exceedingly glad on this account, though now for a little while you may be distressed by trials and suffer temptations, so that the genuineness of your faith may be tested."[7] In other words, tough situations give us opportunities to test whether what we believe is genuine as well as opportunities to find out whether we are genuine about our beliefs.

So what does asking better questions have to do with waging spiritual warfare for the family? Plenty. If we're playing by the rules and living in our roles, but the prince we're kissing looks more like Kermit every day, it's time to stop looking for better answers and put our energies instead into re-examining our presuppositions about what it means to live and love in a world where all have sinned and come short of the glory of God.

Thinking It Through

1. Have you ever been "painted bad" by someone who was secretly sinning against you? If so, what effect did this have on your soul? Have you recovered? If so, how?

2. How do you define spiritual warfare? How do you wage it? What lasting results have you seen?

3. Which problem do you seem to run into over and over? How have you tried to deal with it? Which cherished belief seems to prevent you from finding a solution?

SIX

Some Drink at the Fountain of Knowledge; Others Only Gargle

The unexamined life is not worth living.

Socrates

The mind of the prudent is ever getting knowledge and the ear of the wise is ever seeking, inquiring for and craving knowledge.

PROVERBS 18:15, AMPLIFIED

Fumbling in the darkness, I grab the insistent phone.

"'Lo," I mutter.

"Is this Laurie Hall?" an inquiring mind wants to know.

"Mmmm," I answer.

"I have a friend who needs your help," the voice says. "She just discovered her husband has been involved in cybersex and she won't forgive him."

All seat backs and tray tables suddenly flip into their upright and locked positions.

"Sounds like a smart woman to me," I respond.

"But if she doesn't forgive him, he can't get well." The voice is urgent now.

"If she forgives such a profound betrayal of trust in just a few days, she won't get well and neither will he."

"But Christians are supposed to forgive." The voice sounds genuinely confused.

Somehow, I don't think I'm meeting her expectations. I try another tack.

"Forgiveness is a choice—a choice based on telling ourselves the truth about what has happened to us. It's a process, not a product," I tell her. "Shaming your friend into forgiving because it's something good Christians ought to do robs her of the freedom to choose it."

"Well, how can I be a good friend then?"

Now we're talking.

The woman who made the late-night call for advice on how to help her friend had the best of intentions. She wanted to save her friend's marriage. When we discover that friends are having problems with their marriages, we often take one of two approaches. We either tell our friend to leave the jerk because she (or he) doesn't deserve this grief, or we urge our friend to hurry up and forgive (translation: don't get all emotional about this thing) because we mistakenly believe forgiveness will magically make the nightmare go away. Both approaches are deadly in terms of personal integrity and relational healing.

Rather than repairing the pain that has been caused in a marriage, these common non-solutions abandon both the marriage and the individuals in it because they encourage abandonment of our fondest hopes and highest ideals. Both immediate departure and long-term denial are the refuges of people who lack the courage to ask the hard questions about what it means to live and love with integrity in a world where relationships are frequently torn apart by evil.

Some Drink at the Fountain of Knowledge; Others Only Gargle

The woman who made that late-night call wanted answers for her friend. When we or someone we love is hurting, we just want the pain to stop. So we try to find answers. But, as I have said earlier, the key to healing is found not so much in finding the right answers as it is in asking the right questions.

In his book *Making Sense Out of Suffering*, Peter Kreeft says there are only two kinds of people in the world—the wise who know they're fools and the fools who think they're wise.[1] Kreeft divides fools into two categories: dogmatic fools who think they have all the answers and skeptical fools who think there are no answers.[2] Dogmatism, says Kreeft, is intellectual pride, while skepticism is intellectual despair.

Fortunately, there is a way out of both dogmatism and despair. It is the way less taken, probably because it requires humility, which isn't something we humans get too excited about cultivating. Humility says, "I don't know everything yet. I am open to learning more. I am open to growing more." Humility gives us the freedom to question our presuppositions.

Asking questions means we have to think. Thinking is the way we discover reality. Reality has laws—natural laws that cannot be broken. As we step back and become an observer of our situation, rather than being merely an actor in it, we are freed up to recognize the natural laws which are operating in our situation. Identifying the natural laws that are in operation gives us clues that help us understand the bigger picture. Proverbs 4:26 counsels: "Ponder the path of thy feet, and let all thy ways be established."

Pondering means thinking. I know I'm repeating myself here, but thinking is a lost art. If we are going to climb out of the hole we're in, we have to recover the ability to think. Peter Kreeft says, "Thought is important because it is not just subjective, not just a process inside our heads, but it allows us to live in reality, in truth. Thought contacts truth, however fitfully. It opens our inner eyes to the light. God is truth. God is light. God is ultimate reality. Therefore thought is a lifeline to God. That is its ultimate purpose."[3]

This is why the battle is always for the mind. This is why we are "transformed by the renewing of our minds." This **is** why we have to "take every thought captive."[4] This is why the ultimate meaning of "glory" is recognizing a thing for what it is. This is why fantasy, which says we can create our own reality, is so damaging.

Yet we live in a world where fantasy is encouraged and thought is discouraged. Why bother to think if, as we are constantly told, truth is subjective? Reality, we are informed, is only a matter of interpretation. According to conventional wisdom, there is no such thing as a lie, only different versions of reality. It all depends on what your definition of "is" is.

Madness Takes Its Toll—Please Have Exact Change

People who would keep us from discovering truth spin our perceptions of what has occurred until we are so woozy, we forget the point. How's this for spin control? David Kendall, attorney for President Clinton, in explaining why Monica Lewinsky remembered having sexual relations with the president while the president didn't remember having sexual relations with her, said, "It may well be that people's recollections differ. That does not mean one is lying."[5] Huh?

This, in its rawest form, is the deconstructionist view that truth is a matter of interpretation. If David Kendall and the deconstructionists are right and there is no way to know what "is" really *is*, then there is no way to be connected to reality. Pardon me, but isn't a lack of connection with reality the definition of insanity? If you've ever thought there was something wrong with you for thinking some things REALLY are true and some things REALLY are false, comfort yourself with this thought: You're not the one who's nuts.

OK, so what does this have to do with learning to ask the right questions? Well, if Ken Starr couldn't nail down what was true and what was false when he had an act of Congress behind him, unlimited funding, subpoena power, and a virtual army of lawyers at his disposal, realize that there is no way that you, the average person, can unravel deceit.

Yet, "The spiritual man tries all things[—that is,] he examines, investigates, inquires into, questions, and discerns all things.... Who has known or understood the mind of the Lord so as to guide and instruct Him and give Him knowledge? But we have the mind of Christ, the Messiah, and do hold the thoughts, feelings and purposes of His heart."[6]

Are We Asking the Right Questions Yet?

Fifteen years ago, I lay on my family room floor, weeping before the Lord. I had just received my rainbow mug and after remembering that the rainbow was a sign of the covenant God had made with Noah, I had decided to look in the New Testament to see if the concept of covenant was mentioned there, too. The only book I could think to read was Acts because it contained the record of the early church. If covenant was important to the Christian, I figured it would be mentioned there. I read through the entire Book of Acts in one sitting and then I fell on my face, sobbing into the carpet. I'd never done anything like that before.

But I couldn't help myself. I was completely undone by what I'd just read. That morning, I discovered men and women whose lives were so transformed by their encounters with Jesus Christ that they went out and blew up their culture for God.

"God, I don't have what these people had," I prayed. "And I can't figure out what's missing. I don't have any question that I'm one of Your children; I know I'm born again. But I don't know what I've been saved from or what I've been saved to. Salvation's got to be more than fire insurance."

As I paused to blow my nose, I remembered seeing a "Jesus is the answer" bumper sticker on a car the week before. *If Jesus is the answer, what's the question?* I wondered.

Moving From the Place Where We Are to a Place We've Never Been but Need to Go

On that day so many years ago, God intruded on my life and took me from the place where I was to a place I'd never been but needed to go. He did the same thing to the prophet Ezekiel. Perhaps you remember the story in Ezekiel 37. Let me quote the first three verses for you.

> The hand of the Lord was upon me, and He brought me out in the Spirit of the Lord and set me down in the midst of the valley, and it was full of bones.
>
> And He caused me to pass round about among them and behold, there were very many human bones in the open valley, and lo, they were very dry.
>
> And He said to me, Son of man, can these bones live? And I answered, O Lord God, You know![7]

This story opens with God putting His hand on Ezekiel to move him from the place where he was to a place where he had never been but needed to go. The place where Ezekiel needed to go was a valley. The word for valley in this passage is *biquah,* meaning to cleave, rend, break, or rip open. That's how

valleys are often formed. Some irresistible force, like a giant glacier or a powerful earthquake, rips a mountain apart, leaving behind a pile of rubble. That's
pretty much how our personal valleys are formed, too. Some irresistible force
plows into us, rips us apart, and exposes our guts.

Because the gash is so nasty, we like to run away from the valley and never
look back. Or, hoping others won't notice, we play Fig Leaves R Us and
throw some grass and bushes over the naked parts. But God says every valley
shall be lifted and filled up and every mountain and hill shall be made low, and
the crooked and uneven shall be made straight and level, and the rough places
a plain.[8] Therefore, He meets us in the valley of the mountain we used to be,
and takes us into the places where we've been hopelessly ripped apart so He
can restore our souls.

The Father knows the journey into that dark valley is pretty scary, so at the
get-go, He puts His hand on us. The Good Shepherd scoops the wounded
lambs into His arms and snuggles them right up close to His great heart. The
eternal God is our refuge, and underneath all the trauma are the everlasting
arms.[9]

How we need those arms! When we're suffering, when we've been
cleaned out by some trauma, we feel so alone, so isolated. And then,
Someone touches us. Touch connects heart to heart. Nothing needs to be
said. Words are poor containers for the groanings of our hearts—too confin-
ing, too shallow, too empty. Touch speaks deep to deep.

Picked Over and Dried Out

The valley God took Ezekiel to was full of bones. You don't find bones unless
there's been a death and the vultures are done picking the body over. To add
insult to injury, these bones had been bleaching in the sun for a long time.
Sounds like a hopeless situation to me.

Hopelessness happens when you've given it your best shot, and your best
shot wasn't good enough. That's what happened in this valley—a mighty
army gave it all they had and lost big time. God brought Ezekiel in to see the
devastation. He didn't just show Ezekiel the mess, He made him walk around
in it. Then, God asked Ezekiel to consider the possibility of a new perspective
on the situation.

See, there's the thing that we *do* know about our situation (Ezekiel knew the valley was full of very dry bones), and it's awfully easy to think that the thing we do know is all the truth there is. BUT there are also the things we don't know yet. We don't know those things yet because of ignorance, or because of denial, or because of deception, or because it's not time to know them yet.

To raise the possibility of a new perspective, God asked Ezekiel a question. "Son of man, can these bones live?" Ezekiel answered, "God only knows." (Do you ever feel like that? I sure do.)

The Power of the Question

The point of the question was to challenge Ezekiel's mind-set. When you have a mind-set, you expect things to be a certain way. Kind of like driving on a familiar road and all of a sudden realizing you don't remember traveling the last five miles. We become mindless about the road when we operate under the assumption that we know what lies ahead.

The same thing is true for how we view our lives. We see things in the same dull colors we have come to expect. We formulate our responses to situations based on our previous experience with those situations. We assume that our previous experience is the way it is, world without end, amen. When we operate under assumptions, we become mindless.

Mindlessness causes us to give up choice because we tell ourselves that things are as they always have been and always will be. So, what's to choose? Giving up our right to choose means we paralyze our free wills. Your will can't be free if you don't think you have a choice. This is why it is so critical to renew the mind. We will never know how free our will is until we start challenging our mind-sets.

That's why Jesus often taught by asking questions.

"Do you want to be healed?"
"Who do men say that I am?"
"What seek ye?"

Jesus didn't ask questions because He needed answers. He knows what's in the hearts of men. Jesus asked questions to confront His listeners with their lives, their deepest needs and longings, and the truth of what was in their hearts. As He did, He always invited them to reconsider things in the light of His power, His presence, and His peace.

Here, in this story about Ezekiel and the dry bones, God is doing the same thing. Why? Because Ezekiel needed a fresh perspective on the situation. See, God was about to invite Ezekiel to be part of His plan to put these bones back together, breathe His life into them, and give them back what they had lost. It's no different today. God is still in the restoration business. And, just like in Ezekiel's day, when God invites us to be part of His plan to put the pieces of our lives back together, He starts by leading us to question our presuppositions.

So, let's refresh our perspectives by going back to the story at the beginning of this chapter—the one about the late-night call in which the woman on the other end of the phone wanted her friend to forgive the erring husband immediately upon discovering his infidelities. Rather than trying to come up with pat answers for how this woman can help save her friend's troubled marriage, why don't we walk around the dry bones for a while and as we're looking at the devastation, ask the question, "What is forgiveness, anyway?" Because I have a hunch that, just like He did with Ezekiel, God wants to give us an attitude adjustment so He can invite us to participate in what He's about to do.

Thinking It Through

1. Do you daydream a lot about what life could be like? If so, how is engaging in fantasy keeping you from touching on the painful reality of what really is?

2. When you've done something that you know is wrong, do you ever find yourself lying to cover up the truth? What usually happens when you do this?

3. Where have you given it your best shot only to find out your best shot wasn't enough? How has hopelessness caused you to give up your choice about how you're going to handle your problems? Name two questions you need to start asking yourself.

PART TWO

Dealing With
the Inward Realities

SEVEN

Dust:
Mud With the Juice Squeezed Out

I found that the more I rowed, the more I forgot the directions that had been given to me.[1]

Leo Tolstoy

So God created man and woman in His Own image, in the image and likeness of God He created him; male and female He created them. And God formed man from the dust of the earth and breathed into his nostrils the spirit of life and man became a living soul. And God approved him completely.

GENESIS 1:27, AMPLIFIED

In the beginning, before the ages of time and reaches of space, God created the heavens and He fashioned and formed the earth.

Now, the earth was an empty waste, without form or purpose, and darkness hid the face of the very great deep so that its potential was as yet unknown and unknowable.

In the midst of the meaninglessness, the Spirit of God was moving. Hovering over the waters, He dispelled the smothering darkness and covered the face of the waters with Himself. He brooded there until a reflection of His brightness began to shine back from the waters. And then the Word, which was with God and which would one day become flesh and dwell among us and call Himself the Light of the World and the Living Water, spoke and said, "Let there be light." And there was light.

And God scrutinized the light, and saw that it was beautiful and delightful. He carefully made a distinction between the light and the darkness, between that which gives life and that which chokes it out, between that which reveals His glory and that which hides it. And God called the period of time which was not darkness "Day," and the time of obscurity "Night." And the evening and the morning were the first day.

And thus it went, day after day.

In an explosion of joy, some of the waters sprang up and He caught them and vaulted the heavens. And it was very good.

On the earth, He collected the waters and from their midst raised the dry land. And He admired it.

And the Song of Songs sang into the barrenness of the land, coaxing forth the tender vegetation, and the plants yielding seed and the fruit trees. And He approved them.

Then, the Bright and Morning Star said, "I am not content to leave the Night a time of hiddenness. Let us make it a time of cheerfulness and a reminder of My provident care." So, He scattered bright luminaries throughout space. To some of them He assigned certain paths so that from earth they made pictures of bears and fish and serpents and other interesting things that would mark the days and the seasons and the years.

"I am too generous to leave earth with only crumbs of light twinkling from far, far away," He said. So, God created a greater light and a lesser light. Authorizing the greater light to rule the day and the lesser light to rule the night, God set them in the expanse of the heavens so that at no time would the earth be without light. And He saw that it was fitting and pleasant.

Then, God created the great sea monsters and every living creature that moves, which the living waters brought forth abundantly according to their kinds, and every winged bird according to its kind to fly over the earth. And He delighted in them.

And the Song began its second verse, and the wild beasts and the domestic animals and everything that creeps on the face of the earth sprang forth. And God saw that they were good.

Then, God said, "Let us make mankind in Our image, after Our likeness; and let them have complete authority over the fish of the sea, the birds of the air, the beasts, and over all of earth, and over everything that creeps upon the earth."

And God formed man from the dust of the earth and breathed into his nostrils the spirit of life, and man became a living soul. And God approved of him completely.

And God planted a garden toward the east, in Eden, which means Delight, and there He put the man whom He had formed. And out of the rich soil of that garden, God drew every tree. And in the center of this delightful abundance, He planted the Tree of Life whose fruit would revive from sickness and quicken from discouragement and whose leaves would be for the healing of all people. Also in this lovely garden, He planted the Tree of the Knowledge of the Difference Between That Which Is Excellent, Beautiful, and Cheerful and That Which Is Mischievous, Malignant, and Deadly.

And the Lord took the man and established him in the garden of Eden to serve it and protect it.

And the Lord God firmly instructed the man, saying, "You may freely eat of every tree in this garden. But do not eat of the Tree of the Knowledge of the Difference Between That Which Is Excellent, Beautiful, and Cheerful and That Which Is Mischievous, Malignant, and Deadly. In the day that you eat of it, you will definitely die."

It Is Not Good

And now, for the first time, God saw something that was not the very best that it could be. "It is not good that the man should be alone in such a delightful place," He said.

So, God called forth wild beasts and living creatures of the field and every bird of the air, and brought them to Adam saying, "I'm interested in what kinds of names you can come up with here." So Adam gave these creatures names like "cow" and "elephant" and "platypus" and "iguana" and "eagle."

And Adam noticed that all the creatures he named came in pairs and he wondered where *his* partner was. But after a long time of naming, there was not found a helper particularly adapted for Adam.

So, God said, "I will create a new creature, one who is just right for Adam and who will complete him. I won't make her out of the water or out of the ground, and I won't simply speak her into being. I will build her from Adam's very essence."

Then, God caused Adam to become very, very sleepy and while he slept, God took part of Adam's side and built it into a woman. And, He brought her to Adam. And together, He blessed Adam and the woman He had made from him, saying to them, "Together, be fruitful. Together, multiply and replenish the earth. And while you are replenishing it, together, subdue it and the vast treasures I have placed within it."[2]

So God created both man and woman in His Own image.

And when Adam saw the woman God had built from and for him, he cried out, "She is the essence of my essence. When I see her, I see myself. Well, not exactly myself. My *self*. Therefore, a man shall leave his father and mother and pursue hard after his wife and they shall be one flesh."[3]

Which being translated is: "What a babe! Thanks, God, I'll take it from here."

Nice Story, Laurie, but What Does It All Mean?

When I am asked by a church to come speak about the subject of pornography, I always cringe. I know what they're hoping for. They're hoping I can come present the facts about how bad porn is and offer a formula for how those in bondage to it can break free so everything can go back to normal.

But friends, *normal* is the problem.

The church does not lack teaching on what "normal" is. We have books. We have seminars. We have seminaries. We have radio and TV programs designed to teach us about the "normal Christian life."

In spite of this wealth of information about the "normal Christian life," there is no difference in bad behavior between Christians and non-Christians. Dr. Henry Blackaby, co-author of the best-selling *Experiencing God*, comments on this disturbing trend, "There are just as many abortions inside the churches as there are outside the churches. There's only a one percent difference in gambling inside the churches as outside the churches. George Barna did a survey of 152 separate items comparing the lost world and the churches, and he said there is virtually no difference between the two."[4]

That's bad enough, but here's the real shocker—when it comes to marriage, which is supposed to be a picture of the relationship between Christ and His church, we're doing much worse than the nonbelieving world. Let me remind you of statistics that appeared in chapter four: "While 23% of the general population divorce, people who consider themselves evangelical have a slightly higher divorce rate (27%). Those who consider themselves to be fundamentalists have an even higher rate (30%). Of evangelicals who divorced, 87% did so after accepting Christ, even though it can be presumed they knew of the Scriptures which discourage it."[5]

Finally, when it comes to sex, which is the sign and seal of the covenant of marriage, we're doing much, much worse than the nonbelieving world. While about 40% of the general population has some involvement with pornography, several studies show that 50% of married Christian men are users. Among the pastors, the figures are startlingly high.[6]

Let's pause here and ask ourselves some questions: "Have these trends appeared out of nowhere, by spontaneous generation?" "Is the fact that so many in the church struggle with addictions a surprise or is it a symptom?" "Is the fact that so many of our marriages are falling apart a symptom that Christians aren't trying hard enough to live by biblical standards, or is it a symptom that we need greater clarity about what biblical standards really are?" "Is the secret sexual hell of so many of our pastors and church leaders completely unrelated to their understanding of 'normal' *[or is it a logical consequence of those understandings?].*"

I could be wrong, but from my vantage point, it seems that many who are addressing these trends see them as either freaks of nature whose mysterious origin is completely unrelated to our understanding of biblical standards or as evidence that Christians just don't try hard enough to live up to those standards. I'm wondering if we can afford to continue to cling to this viewpoint. I'm wondering if we might need to look a little deeper.

I'm wondering if Jesus gave us a clue to the source of our problems when He said the fruits are always related to the roots. "Even so, every healthy, sound tree bears good fruit, but the sickly, decaying, worthless tree bears bad, worthless fruit. A good, healthy tree cannot bear bad fruit, nor can a bad, diseased tree bear excellent fruit. Therefore, you will know them by their fruits."[7]

Because Jesus was right—a healthy tree can't bear bad fruit—and if it's true that the evangelical and fundamental church is bearing an abundance of bad fruit, we need to go somewhere with that observation!

I'd like to go back to the beginning, back to Genesis.

In the Beginning

At the beginning of this chapter, I attempted to record the Creation story. I don't think we're going to get out of the mess the church is in until we get a bit more clarity on what this story is telling us. And, since the Creation story tells us about the fall of man and our need for forgiveness, it's pretty tough to become a radical forgiver—the subject of this book—without sitting for a spell with Adam and Eve.

There are disagreements among the household of faith about the opening chapters of Genesis. For example, there are scholars who question their historical accuracy. While they will admit that these stories have religious value, they assert that the facts attached to the stories are "mythical" or "supra-historical." Jesus, however, had no doubts about the importance of the Genesis record. Check out some of His thoughts on the importance of these chapters in Matthew 19:4-6; 24:37-39; Mark 10:4-9; Luke 11:49-51, 17:26-32; and John 7:21-23; 8:44.

"The book of Genesis, as the introductory book in the account of God's progressive self-revelation to the human race, is crucially important. It is quoted more than sixty times in the New Testament, where this revelation culminates in the person of Jesus Christ. In this way, Genesis provides the historical account of the beginning of God's relationship with man foundational for and essential to a proper understanding of subsequent revelations."[8]

There are a number of principles we can glean from the opening chapters of Genesis that are essential to understanding how the world was designed to operate. For now, I'd like to look at just three:

The First Principle: *Purpose, not roles, is what gives order to chaos and meaning to existence.*

The Second Principle: *God urges us to choose life rather than waste our energy grappling over the difference between good and evil, a practice which He warns will bring death.*

The Third Principle: *Zones of authority are designated by purpose and defined by relationships that are mutually beneficial.*

We'll briefly cover the first principle in this chapter and look at the second principle in chapter eight and the third principle in chapter nine. They sound intimidating at first, but they're easy to explain.

Taking a Look at the First Principle
(Purpose, not roles, is what gives order to chaos and meaning to existence.)

How did God bring order out of chaos? How did He make the meaninglessness meaning*ful*?

In the beginning, when God brought order out of the chaos, He did it by assigning *purpose*. He had certain purposes in mind, so He created forms that would facilitate those purposes. For example, God wanted light, so He created the form of the stars in such a way that they give off energy in the form of light. God had other purposes for the stars. They were to mark the passage of seasons and to give signs of His provident care, so He put them in a certain order. As a result, from the beginning, men have been able to use the stars to figure out when to plant their crops, how to navigate, and how to measure time.

Stars have a certain form because they were created for a certain purpose. I know I said that before, but it bears repeating because the point is that their form was not nearly as important as their purpose. If the form were the important thing, the stars would have a uniformity to them. It turns out that about the only thing that's uniform about stars is the stuff they're made of: hydrogen, helium, and dust. Beyond that, there's a lot of variation in size, shape, and color.[9]

Likewise, when God created the dry ground, He formed it for the purpose of sustaining life. As with the stars, there is uniformity of purpose but no uniformity to the form of the land. We find hills and mountains, valleys and meadows, deserts and rain forests, prairies and plains. And no two of them are alike.

In just the same way, humankind has a certain purpose. God took a big gob of mud, squeezed all the juice out, and turned the resulting dust into a glorious reflection of His own image and likeness. Mankind's form is not nearly as important as his purpose, so God created tremendous variations in form. We have red, yellow, brown, white, and black people. We have tall, short, fat, and skinny people. We have people with straight hair, curly hair, and no hair at all. We have people with blue, brown, and green eyes. Although in *form* mankind comes in all sizes, shapes, and colors, the human race was created for one *purpose:* to reflect the image and likeness of God and enjoy Him forever.

Even when it comes to created things that are almost identical, like snowflakes or the leaves on a particular species of tree, we find some form of individuality if we look carefully enough. God is not a cookie-cutter Creator.

This is the way things were in the beginning. How do we attempt to bring order out of the chaos today? Defining roles, rather than examining purpose, is the most common way we attempt to make our world less chaotic. We say, "You are a parent, that is your role in the family." "You are a child. That is your role in the family." "You are a husband/wife. That is your role in the family." "You are a manager. That is your role in this company." We then assign tasks based on what we think the role should accomplish. The assumption is that if people will stay in their roles and perform their assigned tasks, we will tame the chaos and find meaning (perhaps even joy) in our existence.

In themselves, roles and tasks are not bad. However, when they become the focus of the way we order our world, they cause us to compel uniformity. Uniformity confuses form with purpose.

I Can't Believe It's Not Butter

The other morning, I got a delightful e-mail from a woman I'll call Andrea, who had spent many years following the uniform role expectations only to discover that her husband was deeply involved in secret sin. Andrea wrote:

Laurie, I've collected a lot of books about being the perfect Christian woman in the hopes that my husband would one day just look at me (bathed in a stream of sunlight, with an angelic profile, perfectly attired in a long plaid skirt, ruffled lace blouse, and cameo brooch) and all of a sudden be struck by what a gift he had in me and go down on his knees before me, accepting responsibility for all the pain he'd put me through. All the premarital counseling in the world never addresses what you're going to feel like when everything you worked for and were set up to expect if you both did your part blows up in your face! Why do these books keep telling us how to serve our husbands gourmet meals when they should be telling us how to reflect truth to them?

Andrea, it turns out, has been counseling a friend named Jan, who has also been trying to save her very troubled marriage by conforming to the uniform definition of her role as wife. Andrea continued:

Jan still uses anger to hide her deep disappointments that life is not working out according to the formula that our church promotes (unspoken but known by everyone), which is, namely:

1. Wives stay home
2. Mothers, homeschool "them chilluns"[10]
3. Have a daily quiet time
4. Go to Women's Bible Study
5. Be your husband's dream sex machine
6. Act like you have it all together

If you do all these things, it equals Happy Christian Marriage!

Women like Andrea and Jan aren't the only ones struggling with the confusion between role and purpose in this thing called marriage. Yesterday, I shared Andrea's e-mail with a man I deeply respect. This man is a well-known leader and by all appearances was a USDA-inspected holy man. He could talk the talk and walk the walk.

"I was trying really, really hard to measure up," he told me. "I knew the drill:

1. Provide for my family
2. Lead my wife and children
3. Have a daily quiet time
4. Be part of an accountability group
5. Remember to take the little woman out on dates
6. Act like I have it all together"

But, deep inside, he was, as we used to say in East Texas, "all eat up." "I was in a structure that binds you up; there was no room for grace," he said.

He was afraid to admit that he didn't always know the answers to the problems his family faced because somehow he felt his role as head of his household meant he was expected to be the fount of all wisdom.

He was paralyzed when he considered that he was responsible to lead his wife and guide his children. The weight of that responsibility wore him out. So when his family asked him questions, he was often harsh with them. It was easier to put them back in line than it was to explain why he couldn't give them what they wanted.

Keeping up outward appearances, he descended into the fantasy world of pornography, a place where he had perfect control of outcomes and where there was no risk in relationships. In this safe haven, he was all-powerful, all-knowing, and completely immune from the consequences of his decisions. That, after all, is what fantasy is about. (Fantasy wasn't a new way for him to retreat from the pressure of life; he'd actually found it before he got married, but he mistakenly believed he only went there to tame his sexual desires and he thought that once he had a beautiful wife it wouldn't be necessary to go there anymore. He had no idea that going there was more about running from intimacy than it was about feeling good sexually.)

In order to keep his wife from finding out about his secret life, he got very good at hiding behind his role as head of his house.

"I was really good at flying below the radar," he said. "We can use patriarchy as a bully club to beat our wives into submission so we can continue hiding. If we're untrue to God and to ourselves, we die inside. We use all the right terms. But it's so deceptive. Our marriage, which should be filled with the beauty of grace and compassion, becomes a bunch of rules and a legalized lording over. Jesus said the kings of the gentiles lord it over them, but it shall not be so among you."[11]

I asked him what finally brought him to freedom.

"My wife and two of my children asked me what was killing my heart. I went away for several days of fasting and prayer. I realized that I had to stop looking at myself as a role and start looking at myself as a person. Being a role is death. Being a person is life. What God has done in my life is a microcosm of what needs to happen in the church. We have a crippled church that appears to be healthy on the outside but is rotting on the inside. We think we can see, but we're actually blind. We parade around in our robes of self-righteousness, but the world knows we're buck naked."

Yes, We Have No Bananas

Is one of the reasons we're having so much trouble keeping our marriages together the fact that we sometimes concentrate more on the form of a marriage than on its purpose? Is marriage primarily an institution—or is it primarily an intimacy? Is it a system of government or is it a governing body? Because the relationship between Christ and the church is a picture of the relationship between a husband and wife, whatever answer we get to those questions will have application to the next logical questions, "What is the purpose of the church? Is it an institution or is she a body?" Perhaps we should go one step further and ask, "What is the purpose of the relationship between Christ and His people? Is this relationship to be one of rigid role expectations? Or is it to be one of 'knowing' and 'loving with all your heart, soul, mind, and strength'?"

Keep thinking about these things.

Thinking It Through

1. Where do you think the church is doing a good job of being salt and light to our culture? Where do you think the church is struggling to walk the walk instead of just talk the talk? Where do you think you're doing a good job? Where are you struggling?

2. What is your definition of the normal Christian life? How much of that definition is related to role expectations and how much of it is related to purpose? What roles are you playing? How often do you abandon your true self to play those roles according to others' expectations?

3. In what ways do you use anger to hide your deep disappointment that life is not working out according to the formula your church promotes?

EIGHT

Fig Leaves R Us

Formerly the engagement was over the issue of sin;
presently it is not a matter of good and evil but of natural
good versus God's goodness. We contended for the
quality of things before, but now we are concerned with
the source of things.[1]

Watchman Nee

For the Father judgeth no man, but hath committed all
judgment unto the Son. Verily, verily, I say unto you, He
that heareth my word and believeth on him that sent me,
hath everlasting life and shall not come into condemnation; but is passed from death to life.

JOHN 5:22, 24

Taking a Look at the Second Principle

*(God urges us to choose life rather than waste our energy grappling over the dif-
ference between good and evil, a practice which He warns will bring death.)*

I don't know about you, but sometimes I miss the bigger picture. For
years, I've read the account of the Creation and the Fall and concentrated on the literal details of the story. To wit: God makes the world in six
days. God puts Adam in the Garden of Eden and asks him to take care of it.
God tells Adam not to eat the fruit from the Tree of the Knowledge of Good

and Evil. The serpent deceives Eve, telling her that eating this fruit will make her like God. Eve eats the fruit. She gives the fruit to Adam. He eats the fruit. They know they are naked and so they're ashamed. They pull the Fig Leaves R Us job. God asks who knew what when. Each of them blameshifts. God tells them they're toast. He makes them fur coats. Then, He says, "We're in big trouble here. Man has become just like Us. He now knows how to distinguish between good and evil. If he eats of that Tree of Life, he'll have to live forever in this miserable state." So God drives Adam and Eve out of the garden.

I had all the details down. I just forgot to ask what the story was telling me. Here's what I think it says:

God puts Adam in the most beautiful, wonderful place imaginable and asks him to take care of it. "There is only one thing that will kick you out of here," He says, "trying to figure out the difference between good and evil. Once you get tied up with that, it'll kill you."

The warning was not to avoid trying to figure out what was *good*. Everything in creation was good. The warning was to avoid focusing on the difference between moral good and moral deficiency.[2] We can determine right from wrong, but the difference between moral good and moral deficiency is a much dicier thing. Evil can dress itself up in cloaks of righteousness, and good can just be plain misunderstood. That's why judging good from evil is God's job. To do it right, you have to know the heart of the matter. God is the only one who knows that.

I want to camp on this point for just a moment. I'm not suggesting we accept the pluralistic mind-set which tries to tell us that every value system is as good as every other. There are people out there who are very naive about the long-term devastation their value systems are going to bring into their lives. It is possible to explain the logical consequences of their value systems without disrespecting the people themselves. There are also people out there doing real evil. When these people are confronted about their bad behavior, they often counterattack by charging their accusers of "judging." They tell us that what they do is their personal business and that we have no right to impose our value systems on them.

Whereas the difference between moral good and moral deficiency is sort of a sliding scale, right and wrong are matters of clearly defined points of the law. It is wrong to commit adultery. It is right to respect your marriage vows.

Between these two extremes lies the difference between moral good and moral deficiency. For some, not committing adultery has come to include avoiding an entire range of behaviors that might possibly give the appearance of evil. For example, some don't touch or spend time alone with members of the opposite sex, and some never go to movies because so much of what Hollywood produces is designed to incite lust. These things may be quite helpful. Surely if you never touch a member of the opposite sex, you're not going to commit adultery. However, none of these things quench lust. In fact, they may actually aggravate it, because the unconscious message is that touching or talking to a member of the opposite sex is always related to genital feelings. This tinges your interactions with fear, and lust is rooted in fear. The bottom line is lust can not be overcome by focusing on avoiding evil. Lust is only overcome as you learn how to choose life.

Second, once you start down this road of trying to figure out the difference between good and evil, there is always another thing you can do to make sure you don't commit adultery. This is how the Pharisees managed to take the Ten Commandments and make hundreds of laws out of them. They took the doctrines of men and substituted them for the commandments of God. The Pharisees not only had an extensive rule book defining the difference between moral good and moral evil, they also spent a lot of time judging the motivations of others. If you didn't follow their rulebook, well, you just weren't a holy person. Paul had the Pharisees in mind when he said, "For why should another man's scruples apply to me and my liberty of action be determined by his conscience?"[3]

So, back to the Garden: when Satan promised Eve that she would become "like" God if she ate this fruit, he was tempting her with the prospect of being able to look at Adam and "know" the motivations of his heart. I figure she probably thought, "Now I'll finally know what he really thinks of me." (How little women have changed in umpty-ump thousands of years.)

We know that when Adam and Eve ate the fruit they were stripped naked before each other. All the nuances of their souls *were* laid bare for inspection. There was no place to hide and they found such nakedness killing to their spirits because they could feel each other's judgments.

Why do you think Adam ate the fruit, too? Paul tells us that Eve was deceived when she ate the fruit, but Adam knew exactly what he was doing.[4] So, he must have had a compelling reason. I wonder if it's because Eve suddenly had the goods on him and he felt like pond scum. Out of self-defense, he needed a way to strike back so he ate the fruit so he could get the goods on her. I can hear the exchange now, "Oh, yeah, well don't you even *think* about going there when *you* have this issue." Sound familiar?

Knowing good from evil had made them like God all right, but they couldn't handle the shame. So, they ran for cover. We were never meant to be that naked in front of another human because humans don't have the capacity for love, mercy, and grace that our great God does.[5] When we see weakness, we judge it mercilessly and shame is the result. Humans make very poor gods.

We Can Mean Well and Still Miss the Point

All along, God had been saying, "Look, concentrate on things that give life. Otherwise, you'll end up quibbling over what the definition of "is" is, and it's all downhill from there."

It would be nice to think that mankind got the message and stopped judging each other, but no such luck. Thousands of years later, the Pharisees were busily attempting to earn God's approval and avoid shame by figuring out the difference between moral good and moral deficiency. (I want to link Phariseeism with keeping covenant because they meant well, and so do today's legalists.) They knew that obeying the Law was part of keeping the covenant God had made with Israel, so they dissected it into teeny, tiny pieces, coming up with hundreds of rules and regulations to make sure God's people were choosing good and avoiding evil. "If we're to rest on the Sabbath, that means we can't even dig our toe in the dirt," the Pharisees determined, "because that might be 'work' and then God wouldn't be pleased with us."

The Pharisees constantly argued with Jesus over points of the law. But (have you noticed?) He refused to quibble over the difference between moral good and moral deficiency; instead He kept choosing to give life to those who needed His touch. Sometimes, Jesus absolutely scandalized this crowd.

That the Whole World Might Be Saved
One night, Jesus was at a dinner party given by Simon the Pharisee when a hooker walked into the room. Standing behind Him, she washed His feet with her tears and tenderly dried them with her hair. Then (gasp!), she kissed

them. People were dropping their bagels and lox all over the place.

Simon stood in the corner and smirked. "If this man were really a prophet he would know this woman is a tramp," he said to himself. "Godly men don't have anything to do with hookers. I don't care if he's never been in bed with her, it just looks bad."

Simon judged Jesus and he judged the hooker because they violated his rigid understanding of the difference between moral good and moral deficiency. Simon, of course, missed the point. Jesus came not to judge the world but that the world through Him might be saved. Jesus knows if you are going to save people you have to stop focusing on avoiding evil and start focusing on doing good.

Zip forward to today. Marc ran into some modern-day Pharisees when he finally came clean about his lust. Marc had been masturbating since the age of five. It was how he coped with the pain and loneliness he felt. Porn and prostitution were the next logical progression, and he'd been in that hell for years. When everything came out in the open, he was almost relieved. He went to meet with the elders of his church with fear and trembling, hoping that maybe somebody would finally show him the way out of this darkness.

But the elders forgot that darkness is merely a distance from light and that focusing on beating down the darkness will do nothing to usher in the light. So, instead of offering life, they focused on the difference between moral good and moral deficiency.

"Marc," one of them scolded, "I want you under strict accountability. You're to give account for every penny you spend and every second of your day. I don't want to see you with an extra thirty dollars in your wallet or an extra forty-five minutes to kill out there on the strip where all the adult bookstores and hookers are."

Marc was stunned! This was like being told, "Now, you mustn't be a slave anymore. The way out of the plantation is to have someone else 'massa' you. Your old 'massa' did a terrible job. We'll take over until we beat your lust into submission."[6]

Will this work? Marc was already beating himself all the time. He said later, "What did he think he was doing for me, anyway?"

Contrast Marc's situation with David's. David grew up in the chaos of an alcoholic home. He found his way to Bible school and made something of his life. While there, he met a wonderful young woman and soon they were married. But the stress of married life and trying really hard not to be like his dad caught up with David. Soon, he was carrying six-packs home in his briefcase and drinking them secretly in the basement after work. He'd gargle and swallow breath mints until he thought he'd covered up any telltale scent. One day after about three years of drinking and hating himself, he had one of those moments every addict prays for—God spoke to him and he was miraculously delivered from the desire to drink. It doesn't often work that way, but it did for David.

Anyway, about ten years later, he spent some time with John, an old college roommate who had become a pastor. They'd kept in regular touch by phone but hadn't seen each other face-to-face since they'd graduated from college fifteen years earlier. David had never told John about his alcoholism. During their time together, David blurted it all out and then held his breath, wondering what his old friend thought of him now that he knew the worst.

John wept. "David, I know your heart," he said. "I can't imagine the depth of your pain, if you had to resort to the bottle to silence it."

David told me, "I can't tell you what that did for me. I just broke. He didn't judge my failing! Instead, he sat with me in my pain and shame. The grace he extended brought me healing."

John offered life and freedom by entering into David's heart, whereas Marc's elder offered shame and hopelessness by focusing on the difference between good and evil. It's easy to compare the fruit of the two approaches.

If I left the story here, we'd have a good illustration of what types of ministry are killing and what types of ministry are life-giving. But, as these things go, there's more to this story than first meets the eye.

The Rest of the Story

I know the rest of David and John's story. In giving you the rest of Marc's story, I'm going to cut and paste from other stories I've been privy to. Because while I don't know exactly the secret sin of the elder in Marc's situation, I do know what has happened in other situations I've been involved in. Shakespeare wasn't too far off the mark when he wrote, "Methinks the lady doth protest too much." I've often found that those who are harshest with sinners have their own box of goodies locked in a closet they hope no one will ever open.

Turns out that Marc was the elder's worst nightmare. This elder had his own sexual baggage, but he'd never dealt with the guilt and shame of it. Instead, he had punished himself for his transgressions through a variety of strict legalisms, shutting himself off from his essential humanity so he would never, ever be tempted again. The more he punished himself, the more he struggled with his lust, because lust will not be punished to death.

So, daily, his own inner "massa" beat him black and blue while screaming, "You're a fraud. You're a failure. You're bad." To try and stop the blows, he played the part of holy man to the hilt. Somehow, it never mattered how many curtain calls he received for his performance, because when he would retire to his star-studded dressing room, "massa" was there with the whip ready. "You're a fraud. You're a failure. You're bad." Marc, of course, wasn't told about the elder's "massa" because at all costs, the elder could not let Marc know why "massa" was there. The only thing this elder had to offer Marc was fruit from the Tree of the Knowledge of Good and Evil, because he had never figured out how to eat from the Tree of Life.

John, on the other hand, had a different kind of baggage. Recent baggage. Several months earlier, he had been through an absolutely horrendous situation in his church which had bruised and bloodied him badly. No one had come along to bind up his wounds. Instead, his denominational superiors poured salt all over them. John's inner "massa" joined them, "You'll never make it as a pastor. You're a failure. You're bad."

One night, when his wife was out of town, John, who had never, ever abused alcohol, bought a bottle of bourbon and drowned his grief and shame. He buried the evidence in the bottom of the trash barrel, but when his wife returned she found it. Then she ministered life to him as they wept together over the hell they'd been through.

In the midst of the tears, the Holy Spirit reminded John that grace was the only way to "kill the massa." So, he went to the true Master, who had been tempted, tested, and tried in every point that he had. He remembered his Jesus was a man of sorrows and acquainted with grief and shame. He remembered how Jesus' religious leaders had ganged up on Him. He remembered he didn't have to live up to any human ideal, because he lived in the midst of the gospel of grace. So, when Marc sat in front of him, John didn't have to hide behind the fig leaves of legalism. He had dealt with his shame. Therefore, he was able to open his heart to Marc and say, "Hey, buddy, I have some small appreciation for what you've been through."

Marc's and John's stories make me wonder if we're not missing the point sometimes by focusing on the difference between good and evil. I'm wondering if in our frenzied attempts to cover our own nakedness, we're not a little too eager to get the goods on each other. I'm wondering if, in our desire to avoid sin, we're not making a mockery of the gospel of grace.

Personally, I've found the fruit from the Tree of the Knowledge of Good and Evil to be incredibly bitter. Judging whether someone else's heart is morally deficient or having someone else judge my heart as morally deficient is about the most killing thing there is. Seeking to avoid sin by binding myself up in legalities is a pretty close second. No thanks.

I'd rather eat from the Tree of Life. I eat of that tree every time I remember I'm created in the image of a God who's Love. Perhaps that is why Paul said, "Owe no man anything but to love one another: for he that loveth another hath fulfilled the law".[7] If I'm loving my neighbor, I'm going to choose to do what gives life to him or her. Stealing, lying, coveting, murdering, committing adultery, are out. Honoring is in. The fruit from the Tree of Life is not only much simpler to eat, it's much more delicious. May I offer you a bite?

Thinking It Through

1. What seem to be the biggest issues in your marriage? How do you usually resolve these issues? Do you ever resort to getting the goods on each other as a way to avoid having to confess your own issues?

2. How much of your energy goes into defending yourself from the judgments of others? Have you ever judged others as a way to avoid having to admit that you can't fix their problems? Have you ever judged others as a way to deflect shame from yourself? Have you ever judged others as a simplistic escape from the hurtful effects of their bad choices on your life?

3. Recall a time when you were stripped bare by someone's judgment of your motives. What were your feelings? Was it helpful in healing? How did that judgment affect your relationship with that person?

4. Recall a time when someone entered into your suffering. What were your feelings? Was it helpful in healing? How did it affect your relationship with that person?

5. What type of accountability do you find most helpful?

NINE

After This, All the Rest Is Just Details

I know God won't give me much more than I can handle,
I just wish He didn't trust me so much.

Mother Teresa

Jesus Christ has now entered into heaven and is at the
right hand of God, with all angels and authorities and powers made subservient to Him.... And you are in Him, made
full and having come to fullness of life [in Christ you too
are filled with the Godhead—Father, Son and Holy Spirit—
and reach full spiritual stature]. And He is the Head of all
rule and authority.... God disarmed the principalities and
powers that were ranged against us and made a bold dis-
play and public example of them, in triumphing over them
in Him and in it [the cross].... Therefore ... let no one
defraud you by acting as an umpire and declaring you
unworthy and disqualifying you for the prize, insisting on
self-abasement and worship of angels, taking his stand on
visions he has seen, vainly puffed up by his sensuous
notions and inflated by his unspiritual thoughts and fleshly
conceit.

1 PETER 3:22,
COLOSSIANS 2:10, 15, 16, 18, AMPLIFIED

I don't know about you, but I'm really glad that I didn't live during Bible times. It's not that I wouldn't have loved to see the Red Sea part or watch Elijah call down that fire on Mount Carmel or witness Jesus walking on the water or raising the dead. I'd be up for all that. What I absolutely would not want is thousands of years later to risk having my name coming up in a sermon where somebody was trying to explain to a captive audience why I screwed up.

See, the deal was that if you got to see the miracles, you might just get written about, and I mean in excruciating detail. I'm talkin' right where you're walkin', and if you wandered off the path and did some junk you wished nobody would ever know about—sorry. Some prophet was always hanging around making notes about who's being naughty and nice.

Back then, there were no press kits or handlers. Absolutely no PR. Absolutely zero spin control. So, you blow it once, you've blown it bigtime for all time. People are going to be looking into your underwear drawer forever.

Which brings me to some of my favorite people. The disciples. I like these guys because, like me, they mostly didn't get it. They were always doing stuff like shrieking with fright when they saw Jesus walking on water or planning capital campaigns in the midst of transfigurations or being greedy galoots ragging on the amount of money spent on anointing oil. My kind of guys.

One area where they especially didn't get it had to do with what the campaign for the Kingdom of God was all about. They were always after Jesus to designate them to be a vice president or at the very least an ambassador or cabinet head or maybe Supreme Court justice. In their version of the Kingdom, power was hierarchical. The further up you were on the chain of command, the nicer your office, the better your view, and the more people you had scurrying around carrying out your orders. Maybe you even got your own personal cappuccino machine.

The disciples wanted authority to boss people around, so they were always seeking places of power. They thought that authority flowed from power. Jesus told them that power flows from authority and it's not about bossing people at all, it's about serving them.

The Upside-Down Kingdom

The disciples rightly discerned that the concept of authority was a crucial part of the Kingdom of God, they just didn't understand that Jesus was talking about an upside-down Kingdom where the first would be last and the last would be first and the servant would be greater than the "lord." And who could blame them? They were a captive people ruled over by the great Roman Empire. When Caesar said, "Move it," the only smart answer was, "How fast, how far, how long?" So, it's not surprising that the disciples saw authority as bossing people around.

Jesus took great pains to explain that this was not the way His Kingdom operated. Once, after the mother of the Zebedee boys came to Him and asked to have her sons sit in the seats of authority on His right and left, Jesus told His disciples, "The chairs on my right and on my left are not mine to give. My Father is in charge of figuring that out. Look, you know that the rulers of the Gentiles lord it over them, and those that are highest in the chain of command exercise authority upon those they rule over. But I don't want to hear about it being that way with you guys. If you want to be a big shot in my Kingdom, you have to minister to others. If you want to be the big cheese, you have to serve others. I didn't come down here to have people bow and scrape to me. I came to minister to people and to give my life to deliver others."[1]

Jesus was reminding His listeners that while fallen man tends to view authority more like a ladder where the higher up the rungs you go, the more clout you have, God tends to view authority more like rooms in a house. Throughout Scripture, the Kingdom of God is spoken of as the "house" of the Lord. A family is spoken of as a "house." The words "house," "houses," and "household" are used in various applications about 2,200 times in Scripture. Jesus said, "In my Father's house are many mansions."[2]

When I think of a house, I think of rooms that function as a kitchen or a dining room or a bathroom or bedroom. Each room makes the house more pleasant to live in, and each room is outfitted with certain equipment depending on its use. Of course, it's possible to live in a house with very few rooms or where some of the rooms are unusable or poorly outfitted, but it makes life a bit more stressful.

When we first moved into our 1830 farmhouse, we had a lot of renovating to do. So, for several years we basically lived in one room—the kitchen. It was a big room with a woodburning stove on one wall, the front door on another wall, the stairs on another wall, and a big window on the fourth wall. When we put in some counters, a refrigerator, and a stove, even in such a big room there was just enough space in the middle for our table. None of the other rooms downstairs was renovated, and none of them had heat. So, especially in the winter, everyone was in the kitchen all the time and the only place to sit down was at the table. If I wanted to go from the sink to the stove, I had to ask people to scoot in. If I wanted to go from the stove to the refrigerator, I had to ask people to scoot in. I learned a lot about patience.

It was a great day when we finished renovating the living room and I could fix meals in a more relaxed way and we could shoot the breeze with each other in a more relaxed way. The key here is different rooms, different purposes, different appointments, different enjoyments, all working together to make our life together richer and more meaningful. Which brings us to the next point:

Taking a Look at the Third Principle
(Zones of authority are designated by purpose and defined by relationships that are beneficial.)

Let's return for a moment to those opening passages of Genesis and see what the Creation story tells us about zones of authority. God spoke the world into existence. He didn't just wind it up and then go away. He constantly upholds, maintains, guides, and propels the universe by His mighty word of power. But He doesn't micro-manage His creation. Instead, He works through zones of authority.[3]

We find many evidences that God delegates authority in the Creation story. When God wanted the earth to have light, He didn't say, "I'm Light, so I'm just going to stand in the center of the solar system and shine." Instead, He created a greater light to rule by day and a lesser light to rule by night.[4] The word used here for "rule" means to rule over a dominion. Because God purposes that these be some kind of light at all times, the sun and moon each have separate dominions or zones of authority that they are to rule. They rule those zones for the sake of the beneficial purpose of their zone of authority. In other words, the moon doesn't rule the day, nor does the sun rule the night. They aren't just out there giving light, they're giving light because they have a relationship with the earth that's beneficial to the earth.

Man has a zone of authority that is designated by purpose and defined by relationships that are beneficial, too. God created man in His image and likeness. He makes this point a couple of times because it's inextricably linked to man's purpose. God is the ruler and sustainer of the universe, so He gave His image bearers their own zone to rule over and sustain. God said to Adam and Eve, "Be fruitful, multiply, and fill the earth, and subdue it using all its vast resources in the service of God and man; and have dominion over the fish of the sea, the birds of the air, and over every living creature that moves upon the earth."[5]

Granted, the earth is a mini-version of the zone God rules over, but it's a full-time job for us humans. God didn't give us dominion over the earth so we could exploit it for selfish purposes. Our dominion over the earth is supposed to be beneficial to the earth and its creatures. God told Adam to "keep" the garden. He also told Adam and Eve to use the vast resources of the earth in the service of God and man.

We can learn something powerful about the relationship between zones of authority if we observe the relationship between God and Adam before the Fall. God operated in His zone by creating the universe as well as the earth and all that is in it. He told Adam what his purpose was, and then He fully recognized Adam's authority to fulfill that purpose. For example, God created the animals because He's the Creator, but He brought them to Adam for names because He had given Adam dominion over them. God created Eve to be a helper for Adam, but He let Adam decide what to do with her. Adam is the one who instituted marriage. "For this cause shall a man leave his father and mother and cleave unto his wife and they shall be one flesh," Adam said when he first saw Eve. God said, "If that's the way you want to do it, I'll ordain it."

Down through the ages, God has continued to recognize Adam's authority to establish marriage as the foundation of human society. Even Jesus recognized Adam's authority to establish marriage. He quoted Adam as the authority on marriage in Mark 10:7-8.

In the New Testament, zones of authority are defined by spiritual gifts. "And His gifts were varied. He Himself appointed and gave ... some to be ... special messengers, some ... inspired preachers and expounders, some evangelists, some ... shepherds of His flock and teachers." Why? To benefit others: "His intention was the perfecting and the full equipping of the saints, that they should do the work of ministering toward building up Christ's body (the church), that it might develop until we all attain oneness in the faith and in the comprehension of the knowledge of the Son of God, that we might arrive at really mature manhood, the measure of the stature of the fullness of Christ and the completeness found in Him."[6]

Authority works just fine as long as everyone stays in his or her zone and uses that authority to benefit others. But that's the ideal, and if you're reading this book, you know the real rarely lives up to the ideal. So God set up a protection mechanism called a covenant.

Zones of Authority Are Defended by Covenant

In Bible times, "a covenant was treaty, alliance of friendship, a pledge or an obligation between a monarch and his subjects. Covenants were contracts which were accompanied by signs, sacrifices, and a solemn oath which sealed the relationship and spelled out blessings for obedience and curses for disobedience."[7]

Covenants explain the terms of relationships. For example: I'll defend you against enemy attack by providing a certain number of soldiers, weapons, and horsemen, and you'll till my fields and harvest my crops. Or, I'll loan you money to buy your house, but you have to repay that loan by sending me a check for a certain amount by a certain day each month. Marriage is a covenant where a man and a woman promise to love each other until death according to whatever terms they write into their covenantal vows.

Covenants contain blessings for obedience (you get the money to buy your house) and cursings for disobedience (we repossess the house if you don't make your payments). They remind us we are to consider how our choices affect others, and they contain consequences if we exercise authority without considering how it will impact others.

Larry Murphy, Chairman of the Board of Directors for the Elijah Initiative, the ministry I founded to handle the response to *An Affair of the Mind,* works for the Vermont Land Trust, an organization that understands covenantal authority. Early on, the Land Trust established their purpose for existence. Then they wrote ends policies that gave each job at the Trust a zone of authority that would cover some aspect of that purpose.

At the Trust, each employee has the complete authority to do whatever is necessary to carry out his or her job. Each can design procedures and request funds without having to go through channels. So if there is a calculator or desk that will help Larry do his job better than the ones he's got, he can buy it without having to endlessly justify the expense to higher-ups—and then waiting months and months for the check to be written.

He has complete freedom to design the procedures for his accounting duties. The only time he has to check in for approval is if he is making a decision that will affect other employees or the Trust's customers. Even then, he still has the authority to do his job but only after he has run his procedures by anyone who will be affected so they can let him know what impact his procedures will have on them. After talking with everyone concerned, he tailors his procedures for the greatest amount of good and the least amount of harm.

If someone in the Trust makes a decision that impacts other employees without first doing his homework, that employee is held accountable for how that decision impacted others even though the decision itself might have been a good one. Management, then, functions in an almost judicial capacity because they monitor the boundaries. They act as "oil" to make sure zones of authority interact with each other smoothly. The end result of this covenantal approach to running an organization is that each employee at the Trust operates with both a tremendous amount of authority and a tremendous amount of responsibility. Because employees are required to treat each other with the utmost respect, "office politics" are kept to a minimum and working relationships are generally smooth.

New employees often find this type of "government" difficult and a bit frightening because they have never before experienced having the authority they need to do their job. Instead, they have been used to the hierarchical model where someone above them does all the thinking while they do all the griping and complaining about how management doesn't get it. The covenantal approach is like a foreign language to them.

Once they understand that they're in a house, not on a ladder, they take off. Fully empowered to do all that is necessary to achieve their goals, they are able to release remarkable creative energy in their jobs. As a result, the Land Trust has achieved exceptional success in accomplishing its mission and has become a model for businesses and nonprofits throughout the country.

The Cleavers Don't Live Here Anymore

How do we typically run our homes? Do we allow for zones of authority and empower each other to do each job, taking a concern for how we're impacting each other? Or do we make arbitrary decisions and then refuse to help carry out those decisions, or worse, interfere with each other as we attempt to do our jobs? Or do we sometimes completely abandon our zones of authority for the sake of selfish pursuits? As parents, do we make our decisions about the squabbles of our children based on what's just, merciful, and respectful, or do we abdicate the judicial aspects of parenting?

A while back I heard from a wife whose husband had asked her to homeschool their children. She was trying to do this even though her husband's frequent unemployment meant that they often went without adequate nutrition and lived under the constant threat of having their utilities shut off or losing their home. Of course, there was no possibility that they could afford to hire household help so she had the full responsibility for the care of her home and the education of her children and she was cracking.

This woman had submitted to her husband's leadership to the best of her ability. But she had a headship problem. Her husband was not taking care of his responsibilities. He was giving orders, not serving her. He didn't understand that headship is not lording it over others.

Jesus Christ is the head of the church, a position He compares to being a cornerstone. A cornerstone is a foundation stone. It is the place where the building rests. The husband is supposed to love his wife as Christ loved the Church and laid down His life for her. That means, among other things, that he is to be a resting place for her.

If a woman can rest on her husband and know that he will provide what she needs to carry out her task as keeper of the home, she flourishes and her children's hearts sing. When that rest and provision is not there, her heart is crushed and it becomes increasingly difficult for her to mother her children and care for her home.

Like irresponsibility, selfishness undermines the foundations of authority. Many years ago, we knew a young man who did an extraordinarily good job of caring for his wife. He not only made sure she had whatever she needed to do her job, he went the extra mile and did all the gushy romantic things women just love. But this woman was inordinately self-centered. She enjoyed the things her husband provided, but she ignored him in crushing ways. She spent most of her time off doing her own thing. He regularly came home to a cold, dark house, fixed his own dinner, ate it alone, and went to bed alone. The sadness in his eyes still haunts me.

Sometimes, it's the parents who fail to provide for their children's needs. They expect their children to get good grades at school, but then they refuse to shell out the money for tutoring for a weak subject. Or they're so undisciplined themselves that the children's home environment is too chaotic for quiet study. Perhaps they expect their children to keep the lawn mowed but they fail to provide adequate instruction on lawnmowing techniques or don't maintain the mower. Maybe they want certain household tasks done but they fail to provide proper supplies or explain how best to do the job. And, maybe most devastating of all, they fail to provide blessing for the child's obedience.

God provides the model for blessing our children. Jesus did His Father's will and His Father made a point of telling Jesus that He was a beloved Son, in Whom He was well pleased.[8] We don't know how often God told Jesus how much He loved Him and approved of Him when they were alone together in prayer, but we know that at least twice God gave this approval in front of others. Knowing we have our father's approval is about the most empowering thing there is on earth. Children will do most anything to gain this approval. When it is withheld, their spirits are crushed and they have a very hard time feeling secure. The unblessed child is a bad decision waiting to happen, because, he tells himself, if my father doesn't believe in me, why should I believe in me? The blessed child almost always chooses to do what is right, because he knows if his dad believes in him, he is really OK and is able to handle the challenges of life.

Eddy Haskell and Beaver Cleaver Do Church

Sometimes the church gets just as confused about how authority is supposed to work. I am in touch with a young pastor whose denominational superiors asked him to plant a church. He found a building and went at it great guns—there were over 150 people there the first Sunday. Each Sunday saw new faces. No one at denominational headquarters asked him what he needed to effectively pastor these people and grow this church. Instead, they started to pick about the way he was doing things. They didn't like the fact that he put the offering plate in the corner and let people put their money in on the way out. They wanted the plate passed because they felt they would get more money that way. They didn't like the fact that he was meeting in a storefront. They thought he should find something more suitable, even though the rent on his present facility was next to nothing. He is starting to lose his zest for the ministry.

Some churches, on the other hand, do an amazingly good job of understanding zones of authority. Recently, we started attending a new church. We had been looking for quite a while and hadn't found a "fit." The first Sunday at this new church, we arrived at the end of the service, just as they were getting ready to take communion. I had checked the time for the start of the services in the yellow pages ad, and had only noticed regular hours. I hadn't paid attention to the fact that they were now on summer hours and therefore starting an hour earlier.

To make matters worse, this Sunday, because it was so beastly hot, they were meeting outside, so everyone saw us coming. As we approached the group, we realized that we were walking into the middle of things. We had one of those "uh oh" feelings, not knowing whether it would be better to attempt to vanish into thin air or turn around and quickly walk back to our car, hoping our poor timing hadn't interrupted things too much.

Immediately, someone came up to us and made us feel welcome. He showed us where to get into the communion line and gave us a hymnbook already opened to the song the congregation was starting to sing. The first thing I noticed, after getting over my embarrassment, was the joy on people's faces. One older man practically skipped back to his seat after taking communion.

After the service, people came up to us and did much more than just say, "Hi, my name's So-and-So. What's yours? This your first Sunday? Glad to have you with us." Instead, we engaged in significant small talk and actually learned some things about the people. On Tuesday, we received a call from a member of the congregation welcoming us to the church. She wanted to know if we had any questions and left her number in case we thought of something later.

The second Sunday we were there, when we went up to take communion, the rector called us each by name as we received the host from him. "Steve,

Laurie, I'm so glad you're with us. This is the body of Christ which was given for you." Again, after the service, we had several people come and engage in significant small talk with us. One woman took us on the cook's tour of the place and kept saying things like, "This is your kitchen. This is your library. This is your fellowship hall." She told us we could be involved as much or as little as we wanted in the church and still be accepted.

The third Sunday, someone had made lovely name badges for us. The bulletin listed a book group that met at Jim and Polly Larkin's on Wednesday nights. I was interested in attending it as a way to get to know people and learn a bit more about the church. So, after the service, I asked someone about it. His face immediately lit up, "Oh, the Larkins," he said. "They're wonderful." I asked him if he attended the group and he said, "No. But you'll love the people in it." He then introduced me to several of the group members, one of whom offered to get me a copy of the book they were reading. Someone else took me down to the church office and gave me a church directory so I'd have the Larkins' number. Someone else drew me a map showing how to get to their house.

That Wednesday, I had errands to run before the meeting, so I left our home many hours before the group started. An apologetic Polly greeted me at the door. Jim was sick, she said, and they had decided to cancel the meeting. She had heard that I might be coming, and she told me what she had done to try to get in touch with me to let me know things had been called off. We had not filled out any paperwork, so there was no record of our phone number. She knew my name, but our phone number is not listed under my name. She called person after person until she found someone who knew Steve's name, and then she left a message on our voice mail telling me the meeting was canceled.

I was truly touched that she would go to so much trouble for a stranger. I told her about the way the man I had asked about the group had lit up when he spoke of her and Jim. Then she said, "We arrived at this church many years ago, greatly in need of acceptance but feeling very unacceptable." I asked her what the secret of the church was. She said, "We have a wide diversity of people. Young and old. Rich and poor. Educated and uneducated. Very liberal and very conservative. We enjoy listening to each other's viewpoints and learning from each other. We focus on what we have in common, not what we disagree on, and nobody has to prove anything to anybody. You are accepted as you are."

In the weeks since, we've discovered another of their secrets. The leadership of this church believes in empowering people for the work of the ministry. They ask people what they need to do their job rather than telling them how to do it. They see themselves as a resting place for the congregation, rather than as command central. As a result, many of the members are joyfully involved in ministry and the congregation owns the mission of the church.

Lost in Space

Why am I including information on zones of authority in a book on forgiveness? Because sin is a violation of zones of authority. Somebody trespasses on somebody else's zone. Somebody goes into someone else's room and tells them how to rearrange the furniture. Jane takes something that belongs to Sue. A gossip steals someone else's reputation. A man rapes a woman, violating the authority she has over her body. A father tears down his children's self-respect, effectively stealing their personhood. A mother abuses her daughter, violating the authority the girl has over herself. A woman treats her husband poorly, dishonoring his position as head of the home. A man tries to micromanage his wife, thus undermining her competence and position.

Here's a typical situation: A man, after years of masturbating to pornography, begins ogling women at strip clubs or hiring escorts or becoming sexually involved with an acquaintance, thus inviting other women to occupy the place that only his wife has the covenantal right to occupy. He gives these "other women" valuable and foundational resources of time, money, and energy that should be going into making a resting place for his wife. Having sexually violated his covenant with her, he now begins to push her out emotionally with mind games, criticism in front of the children, and competition for the children's affections.

The children become confused about "where" their mom belongs. They intuitively sense she's been kicked out of the club. So they lose respect for her, and they take up the battering ram. They stop obeying her and begin to lip off to her. The woman feels as if she's getting it from all sides and either begins to defend her position as wife and mom or to shut down and stop doing the things that were part of her zone of authority. I have never known of a situation where a husband was involved in sexual sin where he didn't attempt to emotionally batter his wife out of her covenantal place.

This feeling of being "lost in space" is part of the emotional wallop of sin. This sense of "lostness" isn't imaginary, although it's invisible. How exactly do you define the "place" you occupy? How do you know where the boundaries are and what constitutes violation of those boundaries?

Covenant is God's mechanism to facilitate forgiveness because covenant tells us what our place is, whether someone has or hasn't stuck their hairy toe over the line, and what our recourses are.

The Ark of the Covenant: Law, Rod, and Manna

The Old Testament Ark of the Covenant was a very visual reminder of the place of covenant in forgiveness.

Once a year, the high priest would go alone into the Holy of Holies and sprinkle blood on the mercy seat as a way of atoning for the sins of the nation of Israel. The mercy seat rested on top of the Ark of the Covenant. Inside the Ark were several important items. The first was the two tablets of the Law that Moses had received on Mount Sinai.

The law. Whenever I've seen an illustration of these tablets, the artist has drawn them with the four commandments that have to do with our relationship with God on one tablet and the six commandments that have to do with our relationship with man on the other. A Jew recently explained to me that this may not be the way it really looked: it is thought that each tablet might have contained the entire Ten Commandments, two identical renderings of the Law. This is because matters of covenant require two or three witnesses to establish the terms of the covenant. According to this theory, God followed the commonly accepted procedure for covenantal relationships by providing two copies of the Law because the Ten Commandments are the terms of the covenant between God and His people.

The Law is basically a short course in forgiveness because it tells us what debt we owe others and what debt they owe us. It helps us understand the boundaries in our relationship with God and man so we can determine when we're trespassing or when someone is trespassing against us. In the Old Covenant, the Law was external. In the New Covenant, we find the law written in our hearts, where it operates kind of like an internal security system, sounding the alarm when boundaries are being approached. You've probably had that sense you were about to step over someone else's invisible boundary line or that uncomfortable awareness that someone has just stepped over yours.

The rod. Along with the tablets of the Law, the Ark of the Covenant contained Aaron's rod that budded. You may remember the story. People had been griping and complaining that Moses and Aaron shouldn't have all the say-so. "You're taking too much on yourselves," they grumbled. "Everybody here is holy. Who made you guys head honchos?" God was just a tad upset with their arrogance and what happened next wasn't pretty. The earth opened up and swallowed the ringleaders of the mutiny, after which a plague took out another 14,700 people. Then God set up kind of a show-and-tell.

In those days, each tribal ruler led his group with a rod that had been fashioned from the branch of a tree. The rod symbolized the ruling authority of the prince. Sometimes the rod was extended like a scepter, and it also functioned as a walking stick. As a result, it came to represent that which supports life, and therefore figuratively the rod also symbolized "bread" because bread is the staff of life. Since the controversy was about who should get to be the leader, God told Moses to have all twelve of the princes of Israel scribble their names on their rods and then bring them to the tabernacle of witness. "Look, I'm sick of this jockeying for position. You come back tomorrow and check these rods out. The guy I pick to be leader will find his rod budded," God said.

Sure enough, the next morning, Aaron's rod had not only budded, it was producing almonds.

God told Moses to put this rod in the Ark of the Covenant as a sign to gripers and complainers that there are designated zones of authority in His Kingdom.

What does this story have to do with forgiveness? Someone was trying to kick Aaron out of his place. They trespassed against him (and God) by trying to make Aaron think God didn't see him as anything special and that he had no right to be doing what he was doing. This is the way evil works. It seeks to deprive us of our places by shaming us for thinking we ever had the right to exercise the authority necessary to occupy them. Such shaming destroys our passion for life. God defended Aaron's place and authority and restored his joy by giving a visible sign that He approved of him.[9] In the rod, we are reminded that an essential part of forgiveness is reconnecting with our authority and recovering our passion for life.

The prophet Ezekiel compares the rod of authority to the branch of a vine.[10] That's an interesting word picture, especially when you consider that Jesus used this same analogy to remind His followers that God approved of them and granted them Kingdom authority. He said, "I am the vine, you are the branches: He that abideth in me, and I in him, the same bringeth forth much fruit [just as Aaron's rod brought forth fruit]: for without me you can do nothing [but through His authority, we can move mountains]."[11]

So not only did God show His approval of Jesus' message through miraculous signs and wonders, He showed His approval of the apostle's message the same way. As they proclaimed the message of the kingdom of God, the lame walked, the dead were raised, the captives were set free, and many were healed. Truly, their rods "budded" in the presence of those who doubted their authority to proclaim that Jesus Christ is the Son of God who has come to take away the sins of the world.[12]

The manna. Finally, the Ark of the Covenant contained a golden pot of manna, that miracle food that God provided six days a week while the Israelites wandered through the Wilderness of Sin. What does the bread have to do with forgiveness? The Israelites needed physical bread because their bodies were hungry. After 400 years of slavery, they had been robbed blind and didn't have any way to provide for their daily needs. By including the manna in the Ark, God was reminding His people that He is fully aware we need to have our practical needs filled. We are hungry because of sin.

Jesus connected this with forgiveness from sin when He told His followers, "Your fathers did eat manna in the wilderness, and are dead. [I am] the bread which cometh down from heaven, that a man may eat thereof, and not die."[13] Jesus was saying that the forgiveness He offers contains something far more powerful than merely getting our physical hungers met. Our souls and spirits have hungers. Hungers to belong. Hungers to be significant. Hungers to be loved. These are the things of which we are robbed whenever someone sins against us. These are the places where we need restoration. The abiding presence of the Bread of Life heals us by rebuilding in us the image of the Son of God so we can recover our person.

Perpetual witness. To review: the Ark of the Covenant contained the two tablets of the Law, which help us discern the boundaries of our place; Aaron's rod that budded, which reminds us that God approves of us and gives us the authority necessary to occupy our place; and a golden pot of manna, which symbolizes God's abiding presence and provision for the needs of our soul.

Another interesting point is that God Himself had dictated the design for the Ark, and He had requested that on either end of the Ark there be two cherubim who looked down on the mercy seat. Their presence wasn't just a nice architectural detail. Remember that it takes two or three witnesses to establish a covenantal matter. Between those two golden cherubim, the glory of God rested. That makes three "presences" who were looking down onto the Law, the rod, and the bread when the high priest would come into the Holy of Holies to confess the sins of the nation of Israel. These three would bear witness of the terms of the covenant. And thus the transaction of forgiveness was made.

Thousands of years later, Jesus Christ, our great High Priest, went into the heavenly Holy of Holies and sprinkled His own blood on that mercy seat in order to fully secure our forgiveness.[14] This time it wasn't carved cherubim who witnessed the event, it was real ones. And the forgiveness God offers on that mercy seat is much more than just an "It's OK. It doesn't matter." He offers us a restorative forgiveness whereby we recover our person, our place, and our passion. He reminds us of the importance of the Ark of the Covenant in the prayer He taught us to pray:

Our Father, who art in heaven, hallowed be thy name [The first and third commandments]. Thy Kingdom come, thy will be done on earth as it is in heaven [the law, which is the constitution of the kingdom and explains what the will of God is]. Give us this day our daily bread [the manna], and forgive us our debts as we forgive our debtors [the law]. And lead us not into temptation, but deliver us [the rod] from evil. For thine is the kingdom and the power and the glory [law, rod, and bread] forever. Amen [the witnesses agree][15]

When we pray the Lord's prayer, we are reminding God and ourselves that we are in a covenantal relationship with each other. Under the terms of His covenant with us, we can come boldly before His throne and as long as we honor our part of the covenant, we won't leave empty-handed. Jesus said, "And whatsoever ye shall ask in my name, that will I do, that the Father may be glorified in the Son. If ye shall ask anything in my name I will do it. If ye love me and keep my commandments."[16]

Spiritual Warfare for the Charismatically Challenged

The Ark of the Covenant had enormous power attached to it. It went before Israel in all her battles, and her enemies knew they were toast because somehow its presence guaranteed victory. At one point, the Philistines captured the Ark. There was a great slaughter, and 30,000 Israeli foot soldiers died, among them a man named Phineas. When his wife heard of her husband's death, she went into premature labor and delivered a son she named "Ichabod," which means "the glory is departed from Israel." It was because, she said, "the Ark of the Lord has been taken."

The Philistines took the Ark and put it next to their god Dagon. The next morning, Dagon was on his face. "Just a coincidence," Dagon's priests assured each other as they picked their god up and put him back in his place. But the next morning, Dagon was on his face again, only this time he was broken into pieces. After that, it was all downhill. Tumors. Boils. Plagues. Eventually, they sent the Ark back, filled with golden guilt offerings.[17] Just by its mere presence, the Ark of the Covenant changed things.

What does this have to do with spiritual warfare? The Law, the rod, the bread, and the mercy seat remind us that God's abiding presence comes wrapped in the mantle of forgiveness. When forgiveness is present, amazing things happen. Forgiveness is not only the most powerful weapon of spiritual warfare, forgiveness *is* spiritual warfare. Forgiveness is the way God chose to deliver us from the power of Satan, and it is the way we wreak damage in the kingdom of darkness.

This is because we live in a legal universe. Sin is actually a matter of accounting. When someone sins against us, they owe us a debt. That debt cannot be canceled by us, it can only be transferred. We can forgive in Jesus' name. We can say, "I choose to forgive." We can say, "Father, you forgive them, for they know not what they do," but in and of ourselves, we can't actually cover the debt. Only the Father has legal authority to do that, and He does it with Jesus' blood, which He declares has enough power in it to take away the sins of the world.

Do you want spiritual authority? In God's upside-down kingdom, spiritual authority doesn't come from position, it comes from drinking of Jesus' cup, and that means forgiving offenses. Jesus has all authority because He has forgiven all offenses. He uses that authority, not to take vengeance, but to make continual intercession for us before the throne, asking Father God to restore our place, our person, and our passion.[18]

The gates of hell are unlocked by only one key—the key of forgiveness. If you want to engage in some serious spiritual warfare, try going to the Father and saying, "I choose to forgive him. He doesn't owe me anymore. Now he owes You, and here's my idea for how You can make him pay: help him occupy his place with grace, remake him into Your image, and restore his passion for life." Then put in your earplugs, because forgiveness makes hell howl.

Thinking It Through

1. Read the story of the woman and the unjust judge in Luke 18:1-8. This parable was given as an example of how we ought to pray. What applications could this parable have for spouses approaching each other about something that isn't right in the marriage? (Remember that the relationship between Christ and the church is a picture of the marriage relationship.) What application could this have for a child coming to his or her parent about something that isn't right in the parent-child relationship?

2. Read in John 14:12-14 and Acts 1:8 about Jesus' excitement that His disciples surpass His accomplishments and His eagerness to empower them with everything they will need to do greater things than He did.

   What applications does this have for how spouses should "tend each other's gifts"? For how pastors and congregations should view pecking order versus gifting? For how a wife should respond if she's told, in the name of "submission," not to excel in any area her husband hasn't mastered?

3. Read about Jesus' view of shared authority in John 15:15 and 16:15. What applications do these passages have to the command-control model of hierarchical structures, in which those underneath you in the chain of command are kept in relative ignorance of the bigger picture?

4. Read Matthew 23:1-11 for Jesus' views on hierarchical structures. How are these principles modeled in your church? In your home?

TEN

Grumble, Grumble, Beans, Burgers, and Trouble

We ... have gathered like eagles around the carcass of cheap grace, and there we have drunk of the poison which has killed the life of following Christ.[1]

Dietrich Bonhoeffer

Verily, verily, I say unto you, Except you eat the flesh of the Son of man, and drink his blood, ye have no life in you. Whoso eateth my flesh, and drinketh my blood, hath eternal life; and I will raise him up at the last day. For my flesh is meat indeed, and my blood is drink indeed. He that eateth my flesh and drinketh my blood, dwelleth in me, and I in him. As the living Father hath sent me, and I live by the Father: so he that eateth me, ever he shall live by me.

JOHN 6:53-57

Eighteen seven-day-old baby chicks are peeping and scratching and looking quite cute down in our barn. Of course, they won't be cute for long. Bred to do nothing but eat, these chicks spend their days chowing down. By the time they're ready to become chicken and dumplings, they've gone from sweet and cuddly to downright mean and ugly.

Since we moved to Vermont eleven years ago, we've raised turkeys, meat birds, laying hens, and several head of beef. Because we also plant a good-sized garden, we've had many a meal when everything on our plates has been raised right at home. This adventure in self-sufficiency has given us an appreciation for the reality that in order for us to live, something else has to die. This has been a sobering thought and has prompted us to give excellent care to the animals we raise.

It has also helped us understand in new ways the sacrifice of Christ who died so that we might live and who commands us to eat of His body and drink of His blood.

I don't know about you, but I have been offended by that passage. Offended that Someone had to die so I can live, and offended that I am asked to regularly remember that sacrifice. Offended to think that my sin so violently assaults God's sense of justice that only a violent assault on One who never sinned could balance the scales.

So just as I would prefer to buy my chicken in a store where I have never seen it alive and cute and cuddly, I would prefer to avoid thinking about the crucifixion.

I may not be the only one. To proclaim "He is risen!" Protestant churches usually feature an empty cross. Often, it's made of a nice piece of polished wood or of some precious metal with ornate carvings appropriately placed. A few bravely raise a cross made of rugged pieces of wood, timidly making the point that this was an uncomfortable place to die. We talk about the cross and we talk about the blood of Christ, but we don't like to really see it in all its dreadful goriness.

God, it seems, is not satisfied with my reluctance to gaze on His suffering. In recent months, He has been compelling me to meditate on the cross—to place myself at His bruised, sweaty, dirty, blood-encrusted feet and weep over His love for me. As I have done so, I have discovered a new thing: I have never felt more loved than when gazing at what His love for me cost Him.

Meditating on the cross reminds me that there is One who has truly been tempted, tested, and tried in every point, yet was without sin, and whose very suffering has qualified and equipped Him to be my High Priest and to comfort me when I am being tempted, tested, and tried. In short, I have learned that the way of the cross leads home. I have learned more about forgiveness by simply gazing upon Him than I have understood from years and years of reading about it.

Gazing at the cross brings up some pretty strong feelings. Christians can be highly suspicious of anything that evokes pesky emotions. But we see a cross that says, "Face the pain. I am with you."

If we choose to celebrate the resurrection by having an empty cross, then let us also pause to honor the crucifixion by remembering that cross was occupied by a bleeding, writhing man just three days earlier. In that pause, we are reminded that feelings are part of forgiveness. Stuff like shame, hope, guilt, fear, longing, despair, rage, desire, loneliness, love, tenderness, pity, curiosity, jealousy, regret, confusion, courage, and contempt swirl all around the cross.

This may come as a shock to some. There seems to be a myth that forgiveness can be done with only a modicum of fuss and bother. To wit: first, we feel some feelings, then we try to feel the feelings of the person who hurt us, then we try to understand why they did what they did, then we tidy up whatever stray feelings remain, bury them in the deepest sea, put up a sign that says "no fishing," and go on. Friends, this is nothing but arrogance. If forgiveness could be had so easily, God the Son would certainly have managed to do it in a tidier fashion than being whipped to shreds, having His flesh pierced by spikes, feeling His heart burst apart, and spending three days in hell.

The Courage to Be Real

I don't know about you, but I don't like to show my true feelings in front of someone who's really hurt me. It feels way too vulnerable. I prefer the "never let 'em see you sweat" approach. However, I've noticed that while learning how to control our emotions is an important part of maturity and a necessary skill in business relationships and with casual acquaintances, there's a difference between controlling our emotions and having inappropriate emotions.

Jesus had the courage to be real. No matter whether it was agony at the cross, ambivalence in the Garden, exhaustion after a long day of healing and breaking bread, sorrow in front of a friend's tomb, anger in confronting those who were using religion to rip off others, tenderness with a broken woman, or relaxing at a dinner party, Jesus' emotional response to every situation was totally appropriate.

Sorting through the complex emotions that are part of forgiveness takes time. That runs counter to another myth about forgiveness: We should be able to give and receive forgiveness instantaneously. Somehow, we think there's something badly wrong with us if we're slow about it.

Listen, if forgiveness could be had instantaneously, God wouldn't have been planning our forgiveness from the foundation of the world.[2] Depending on how you count time from the Creation (and if you think I'm going to get into that argument, you've got another think coming), that's a minimum of 4,000 years for God to set the world to partial rights after the Fall.

And here's how He did it: The Word that was in the beginning, through whom the world was created and the reaches of space and the ages of time, took upon Himself the form of flesh and dwelt among us. Jesus could not have forgiven us if He hadn't been God, but He also couldn't have forgiven us if He hadn't been human. By flesh sin entered into the world and by flesh it must be forgiven.

Jesus Christ is called both the Son of God and the Son of Man. So, while He was among us, He thirsted. He hungered. He tired. He raged. He desired. He laughed. In every way, every day from the time He arrived on planet Earth, He experienced what it is to be human while at the same time doing extraordinary things that showed He was also God.

You never see the mix of His humanity and His divinity more clearly than in His passion. The last twenty-four hours before His death, He served. He confronted. He wept. He yearned. He sweat blood. He healed. He stumbled. He fell. He feared. He loved. He cried out. He embraced. He despaired. He persevered. He forgave. He gave up. He overcame. And three days later, He triumphed.

Just in case His disciples didn't get the point that coming in the flesh was an essential part of forgiveness, when He was resurrected, Jesus celebrated by hosting a lakeside fish barbecue. He also asked them to touch His body so they would know it was really and truly the Son of Man standing before them in the Upper Room. Then, just in case they didn't get the point that He was also the Son of God, Jesus walked through walls, raised the dead, and rose up to heaven right before their very eyes.

Do you know what a nexus point is? A nexus point is the place where things are connected. All of Jesus' humanity and all of His divinity connected at the cross. Thus, for Jesus, forgiveness is the nexus point where He is most fully human and most fully divine. If we are going to forgive others, we have to come to that same nexus point. We must connect with the reality that we are human beings who carry within us the very image and likeness of God. We must "let this mind be in (us) which was also in Christ Jesus: Who, being in the form of God, though it not robbery to be equal with God: but made himself of no reputation, and took upon him the form of a servant, and was made in the likeness of men."[3] Being equal with God was not something Jesus had to attain, rob or grasp. It was already His. He knew who He was. Likewise, when we begin to know who we are, when we begin to rest in the fact that we are joint heirs with Jesus Christ, when we live in the truth that those who believe in Him will never be judged, rejected or condemned (John 3:17), forgiveness begins to flow out of us.

Grumble, Grumble, Beans, Burgers, and Trouble

In those grim three days before the resurrection, the disciples did *not* understand the way the campaign for the Kingdom had turned out. Several thousand years earlier, after witnessing a series of special effects guaranteed to one-up Star Wars at the Oscars, the Israelites didn't get it either. They celebrated the two week anniversary of their emancipation from 400 years of slavery by grumbling about the grub they were being served. "Look, Moses, beans and burgers are getting old. In the good old days, we ate prime rib every night. And man, the bread we'd put away. Why'd you bring us out here, anyway? So you could watch us starve? God should have just killed us in Egypt."[4]

So God rained down heavenly bread that tasted kind of like a cross between vanilla wafers and baklava. Then God told Moses and Moses told Aaron and Aaron told the people, "Get out there first thing every morning and gather an omer[5] for each member of your family. That should last you through the day. Don't get greedy and load up on it. If you try to hoard, it'll just go bad on you. Besides, there'll be plenty more the next day. Well, except for Friday. Gather enough then to last through Sunday morning. There won't be any manna on Saturday because I want you guys to have a whole day off." God set it up this way so He could tell if the people were going to walk in His law or not.

You remember the story. Some of them gathered more than they could eat and it went to stinking, and some of them went out on Saturday to gather as usual, only to find nothing in the field. But sure enough, Sunday morning the manna was on the ground again. Anyway, God told Moses to gather up an omer of manna and put it in the Ark of the Covenant so that future generations could see the bread He fed His people in the wilderness. Centuries later, Jesus told those future generations, "I am that bread of life. Your fathers did eat manna in the wilderness, and are dead. This is the bread which cometh down from heaven, that a man may eat thereof, and not die. I am the living bread which came down from heaven: if any man eat of this bread, he shall live for ever: and the bread that I will give is my flesh, which I will give for the life of the world."[6]

Jesus was saying there were striking similarities between the bread in the wilderness and the bread of His flesh, and that somehow those similarities were all tied up in what it means to forgive. And, of course, He reminded His disciples of that again in the prayer He taught us to pray. "Give us this day our daily bread" harkens back to the dailyness of the manna and comes right before the "and forgive us our trespasses as we forgive those who trespass against us" part.

Do you know what the word *manna* means? It means, *What is it?* When the Israelites first saw the manna lying there, they said to each other, "What *is* that?" and the name just stuck. Jesus was just as mysterious. People couldn't figure out what He was about. The scribes and Pharisees regularly asked Jesus, "Who do you think you are?" And He turned around and asked His disciples, "Who do you say that I am?"

Jesus was a walking, talking forgiveness machine. Everything He did modeled a life filled up and overflowing with forgiveness. Only Jesus' idea of forgiveness didn't exactly match up with the prevailing religious dictates of the day. The scribes and Pharisees were always on Him because He didn't fit their model of a holy person. He was just a little too loosey goosey for them. A little too much of a party animal. A little too frayed around the edges to be kosher. The disciples couldn't figure Him out either. They were always after Him to nail down His party platform, pick His cabinet, and plan His inauguration.

The point here is that Jesus walked out forgiveness in a way that had nothing at all to do with phony righteousness or gaining popularity. Jesus didn't have a platform. He never polled the masses to see what trick He could perform, what act of self-sacrifice He could do, what type of credentials He could gain that would make people say, "Gee, He wasn't such a bad guy after all; wonder why we crucified Him?"

Jesus didn't follow a forgiveness formula. No picking out a spotless lamb, slitting its throat with a sharp knife, sprinkling its blood on the mercy seat, and then being done with it for another year. Jesus forgave in a way that was much more direct and much more in the present moment. Jesus forgave with bread. He broke open His own being and within Him was enough to feed the entire world so that no one, absolutely no one, who eats of this bread will ever hunger again.

Spin Patrol

Forgiving with bread required Jesus to make this very messy stop at the cross. If you were campaign manager for someone running for King of Kings and Lord of Lords, is the cross a place you'd stop on the campaign trail? Or would you run it something like this? "Just want to go over today's schedule, Jesus. First stop is Bethany, where You're going to raise Lazarus from the dead. We've brought in a contingent of medical experts so we can fully document the resurrection the moment it occurs. We've also arranged for some well-placed leaks, so the media are already camped out. We'll get some face time on the evening news for this one.

"We're doing lunch in the wilderness to demonstrate your plan for welfare reform. We've got the kid with the loaves and fishes all staked out. At the end of the meal, we'll gather all leftovers into baskets for the photo ops. We want things wrapped up no later than 2:00 P.M. so we can make the deadlines for next week's issues of *Time* and *Newsweek*. Incidentally, to keep the labor unions happy, Pete's going to mingle with the crowd and let it drop that the baskets were made right here in Israel, not in some Third World sweatshop.

"Later in the afternoon, we're stopping in Galilee, where there are a couple of lepers who need cleansing. Make sure the cameras catch You actually touching them—we need to show You're a man who feels their pain. There's a fifteen-minute press conference after the healings. I've got the speech writers busy with some sound bites about how You're willing to reach out to the disenfranchised.

"You've got a forty-five minute break and then it's dinner in Cana, where You're scheduled to change water into wine. This one's a little tricky. It's got to be a good enough wine so that the rich Republicans know You're their man but not so hoity-toity that we alienate the Democrats and the middle class."

With polling numbers high after a string of such astounding campaign appearances, how in the world would you spin the crucifixion? Would you be in front of the microphones saying, "We're standing here in Pilate's court-yard, and our man is behind in the popular vote, but the ballots from the rural precincts where Jesus did most of His miracles haven't been counted yet"?

What about when the final tally was made and even the write-in vote demanded crucifixion? Would you have your spinners telling reporters, "Supporters are gathered here at campaign headquarters, where we're expecting the Kingdom to be ushered in following a last minute appearance by the Supreme Ruler of the Universe, who, as you know, originally per-suaded Jesus to run for office"? What would you do when your man died right there in front of the whole known world? Shut the lights off and go home? You would if you didn't know that forgiveness is a poignant mixture of enormous generosity and utter despair. Let's look at that in the next chapter.

Thinking It Through

1. Which of the emotions swirling around the cross speaks the most to the emotions swirling around in you? Can you remember another time when Jesus had similar emotions? How does entering into the fellowship of His suffering help you process those emotions?

2. What myths have you believed about forgiveness? How have those myths kept you from processing what happened to you?

3. In your journey through forgiveness, have you been consulting focus groups to find out how you can manage your pain in a way that will gain you the most votes for Holy Person of the Year? How has the dishonesty of people-pleasing kept you from healing?

ELEVEN

Lessons From the School
of Abandonment

The praying man not only says, "I can't do it and I don't
understand it," but also, "Of myself, I don't have to be
able to do it, and of myself, I don't have to understand
it." When you stop at the first phrase, you often pray in
confusion and despair, but when you can also add the
second, you feel your dependence no longer as helplessness, but as a happy oneness which looks forward to
being renewed.[1]

Henri Nouwen

My God, my God, why hast thou forsaken me?

PSALM 22:1

R emember Joseph, favorite son of Jacob?[2] He had dreams that one day
his mother, father, and eleven brothers would bow down to him. This
didn't set too well with the bros. "Who does he think he is, anyway? Bad
enough he's daddy's little man—now he wants to lord it over us? Pigs might
fly," they groused to each other.

One thing led to another until the bros decided they would give Little Joe
the attitude adjustment he so richly deserved. As the Midianite slave trader
was leading Joseph off in shackles, the bros chortled, "Dream on, Egyptian
slave boy!"

Joseph's troubles were just beginning. He was sold on the slave block to a man named Potiphar. After years of faithful service, his master's wife falsely accused him of coming on to her, and he was thrown in jail. We don't know how long he was in prison, but we do know that he was thirteen when he was sold into slavery and thirty when he was finally released from prison. That means seventeen years of some kind of misery.

When you read Joseph's story in Genesis, you don't get any sense that he struggled with despair during those seventeen years, but Psalm 105:16-19 (AMPLIFIED) tells the rest of the story.

Moreover He (God) called for a famine upon the land of Egypt; He cut off every source of bread. He sent a man before them, even Joseph, who was sold for a servant. His feet they hurt with fetters, he was laid in chains of iron and his soul entered into the iron; Until his word came true, the word of the Lord tried and tested him.

Did you get that? While Joseph was waiting for God's promises to come true, those chains and fetters didn't just cut into his feet and wrists, they cut into his very soul. The cruel iron mockingly reminded him that he was no longer daddy's darling, no longer someone his family was going to bow to. No. He was a slave—a man without help or hope. He kept remembering God's word to him, and none of what he was enduring made any sense.

Finally, seventeen years after the horror show began, he was released from prison so he could interpret Pharaoh's dreams about seven fat cows being devoured by seven emaciated cows, and seven plump, juicy ears of corn being devoured by seven withered ears of corn.

His interpretation and the accompanying advice didn't free Joseph from slavery, but it did rocket him into the number two position in the Egyptian government. From that position, Joseph greeted his unsuspecting brothers when they came to him years later and fell on their faces before him, begging some grain. Turning his back to them, he wept. Suddenly, it all made sense.

God had done this to him. Yes, his brothers had sold him into slavery, but God had set them up to do it so He could send Joseph before them. God had done this to the Egyptians. He sent the famine and cut off every source of bread. God had done this to the brothers, too. He used the famine to bring them to Egypt. Now here they were, bowing before him, just like in Joseph's long-ago dreams.

But until this very moment, Joseph never would have guessed it would turn out like this. For seventeen long years, he had clutched his dreams in shackled hands while grappling with the apparent contradiction between God's promises and the reality of his present circumstances. As he stood there on that longed-for day and looked down at his kneeling brothers, Joseph realized that joy burns brightest after hope has passed through the dark agony of despair.

Risky Business

Hope requires us to risk trusting that God's Word is true without the foundation of knowing exactly how things will play out or when resolution will occur. Meanwhile, the fetters bruise our feet. The chains cut into our wrists. And our souls enter into the iron.

During those confusing, agonizing years of slavery and imprisonment, Joseph had to keep on keeping on, which takes a *lot* of energy. Often, this energy fills us as we draw on the joy we expect to experience when our hopes are finally realized. We "pre-experience" this joy as we visualize our hopes being fulfilled a certain way. We close our eyes and imagine how happy we will be when our brothers finally accept us, the marriage is restored, the child is healed, or the job promotion comes through. Our hearts soar over the rainbow as we imagine "someday, somewhere." Refreshed by future joy, we dare risk trying a while longer.

When, despite exhausting ourselves with our efforts, we're sold into slavery, the abuse continues, the child dies, or we are downsized, we come face to face with the fact that our hope, as we have so often visualized it, will never be realized. Shaken, we realize there is no pot of gold at the end of the rainbow for us. Hope dies. Joy is aborted. And we enter into despair.

Despair creates a metaphorical vacuum. When we experience despair, everything that isn't bedrock gets sucked into the abyss. This is the great gift of despair: It strips us of that which we think is important in order to awaken us to that which is essential.

Being Left in the Lurch

In the midst of our despair, we may give lip service to Scriptures like Romans 8:28 and tell others that we know God will work all things together for good for those who love Him, but deep inside our hearts, we wonder, *I love God, but does God love me? If God really loves me, why would He let this happen? Why would He leave me in the lurch? Can I ever trust God again?*

Joseph certainly struggled with this. So did Jesus. Two thousand years ago, He hung on a cross and cried in fear and terror, "My God, my God, why have you left me in the lurch?"[3]

Usually, you and I are like Joseph: we don't know why we are suffering through trials or when it will end or how it will turn out. Jesus knew the rest of the story and understood that forgiveness would triumph in the end, *really*. Yet, when He was abandoned at His hour of greatest need, despair pierced Him. It is a myth that radical forgiveness can be gained without piercing moments of hopelessness.

The Gospels do not tell us all that Jesus said as He hung on the cross. It's possible He quoted Psalm 22. Charles Spurgeon says, "This is beyond all others 'The Psalm of the Cross.' It may have been actually repeated by our Lord when hanging on the tree; it would be too bold to say so, but even a casual reader may see that it might have been. It begins with, 'My God, my God, why hast thou forsaken me?' and ends with, 'It is finished.'"[4]

Listen to a few verses from that psalm. Listen to them with your heart, not your head:

My God, my God, why have You forsaken me? Why are You so far from helping me, and from the words of my groaning? O my God, I cry in the daytime, but You answer not; and by night I am not silent or find no rest....

Our fathers trusted in You; they trusted and You delivered them. They cried to You and were delivered; they trusted in ... You and were not ashamed ... or disappointed. But I am a worm, and no man; I am the scorn of men, and despised by the people.

All who see me laugh at me and mock me; they shoot out the lip, they shake the head, saying, "He trusted and rolled Himself on the Lord, that He would deliver him. Let Him deliver him, seeing that He delights in him!" ...

I am poured out like water, and all my bones are out of joint. My heart is like wax; it is softened with anguish and melted down within me. My strength is dried up like a fragment of clay pottery; my tongue cleaves to my jaws; and You have brought me into the dust of death.[5]

Whether Jesus quoted this whole psalm or just the selected verses that appear in the Gospel accounts, His cries of despair are as piercing as the nails in His hands and feet. What does His passion tell you about the reality of forgiveness?

Scripture tells us that after crying out again, Jesus "gave up the ghost."[6] The One who walked on water; the One who raised the dead, healed the sick, and restored sight to the blind; the One who resisted tremendous temptation in the wilderness; the One whose face shone like the sun when He was transfigured before Peter, James, and John ... died when His Father abandoned Him. Being abandoned in the midst of great difficulty is killing.[7]

Do You Want That Toasted or Plain?

In previous chapters, we looked at how the presence of the bread in the Ark of the Covenant reminds us that forgiveness is the nexus point between our human nature and our divine calling. Now, Jesus and Joseph remind us that forgiveness calls us to eat of the bitter bread of abandonment.

Perhaps you've been served a slice from this loaf. My recollection is that it doesn't come with jam or even a decent amount of butter—absolutely nothing to help it slide down your throat before it lands like a bomb in your belly. I don't think you even get to choose if you want white or whole wheat. Nope, someone just rips off a slab and flings it your way.

Perhaps that someone was a husband or wife who walked into the living room one night after you'd done the dishes for the ten thousandth time in your life together and announced he or she wanted a divorce because a new love had arrived via the Internet. And there you were, thinking about how you needed to shop the sale at Wal-Mart so the kids could get their new school clothes or maybe how you needed to change the oil in the car before next month's vacation. You had no idea that Christmas stockings and children's giggles could be stolen in cyberspace.

Or maybe your slice of abandonment bread got served as a nurse tightened the tourniquet around your arm so she could do an AIDS test because your husband just confessed he'd been unfaithful. And as the needle slid in, in your mind you burrowed to the bottom of your grandmother's cedar chest. There, wrapped in tissue paper, is the nightgown you wore on your wedding night. And the ribbons haven't faded and the tucks in the bodice are still as crisp and delicate as they were twenty-five years ago when you gave yourself to your one and only, but now your mind's eye can discern a horrible stain where the bread landed.

Or perhaps the slab is hurled as you sit quaking before your church's board of elders, asking them to help you save your marriage from the newly discovered threat of your husband's involvement with pornography. And they look you in the eye and inform you that he wouldn't have had to resort to glossy pretties if you had been a better wife.

And if he pushed you into the living room wall—what did you do to provoke him, anyway? And you realize that all the chicken pot pies you baked and all the times you washed his underwear and all the times you caught your breath when you looked at him because even after twenty years of marriage the sight of him still turns you on, count for nothing.

There's an ugly twist to this loaf of bread—you don't always get served this bread because you've done something wrong, but often because you've done something very, very right.

Joseph's abandonment to prison and Jesus' abandonment on the cross had their foundation not in their guilt but in their righteousness. Who they were and how they conducted their lives infuriated others. Joseph's decision to stay out of someone else's marriage bed ticked off Potiphar's wife. She took vengeance by having him thrown in prison. Jesus enraged religious leaders who were afraid they would lose market share to His powerful message of God's unconditional love. They tried to silence His message, but He wouldn't get out of their faces. So they crucified Him on trumped-up charges.

In her wonderful book, *Home by Another Way*, Barbara Brown Taylor tells the story of going to a church retreat where the opening exercise was to tell about someone who had been Christ to them. Barbara says one by one people got up and told lovely stories of friends who'd helped through long illnesses and neighbors who'd taken the places of fathers who'd self-destructed. "One after another, the[re] were stories of comfort, compassion, and rescue. The conference room turned into a church, where we settled into the warmth of each other's company. Jesus our friend was there with us and all was right with the world, until this one woman stood up and said, 'Well, the first thing I thought about when I tried to think of who had been Christ to me was, "Who in my life had told me the truth so clearly that I wanted to kill him for it?"'

"She burst our bubble, but she was onto something vitally important that most of us would be glad to forget: namely, that the Christ is not only the one who comforts and rescues us. The Christ is also the one who challenges and upsets us, telling us the truth so clearly that we will do appalling things to make him shut up."[8]

Being Our Own Worst Enemy

The bread of abandonment isn't just about others doing appalling things to us; sometimes we serve ourselves the bread.

For example, it's a good thing to know the difference between justice and injustice because that knowledge shows us how to treat others. It also lets us know when we've been treated unjustly and therefore must begin the process of forgiveness. However, our knowledge of justice and injustice tempts us— what does it mean to overcome evil with good? Does this mean we can't demand our day in court? Or what if we satisfy each requirement of the legal system, yet they let the one who treated us unjustly off on a technicality?

In the same vein, our ability to love lets us know when others are treating us in loving ways and when they are treating us in abusive ways and therefore need to be forgiven. However, our knowledge of the difference between love and abuse tempts us—should we turn the other cheek? Or should we shake the dust off our feet and move on? What if, as we choose to work through deep betrayals of trust by waiting patiently to see if our relationship with the one who wounded us can be healed, we are abandoned by others who judge us as "codependents who love too much"? What if we actually do become enmeshed in codependent confusion? What if, after putting great energy into reconciliation, we are forced to abandon hope for the relationship because the other person chooses not to work things out?

It's a strength to have faith that God hears and answers prayer. Our faith in God causes us to boldly come before the throne and intercede for the needs of the world. Our faith also causes us to persevere in prayer for those who despitefully use us and therefore need our forgiveness. However, our faith tempts us—what if God doesn't love me enough to answer my prayers? Does His delay in answering mean I have hidden sin that needs to be confessed? How many years does He expect me to pray about this, anyway? What is my part and what is His part? What if faith asks me to abandon my hope because God's answer to my fervent prayers is, "No. I have another plan"?

Sometimes our strengths get so warped by our woundedness that they drive us to fill our empty bellies with that which is not bread. Our good desire to be loved, our good desire to belong, our good desire to feel secure, can get so twisted around our pain that we use those desires to justify our search for anesthesia in sex, food, drugs, unhealthy relationships, money, achievement, or some other numbing agent. This is how addictions are formed. Addictions are a symptom that we have abandoned ourselves in our frenzied search for bread.

The Place of Broken Bread and Spilled Out Wine

Dietrich Bonhoeffer said,

> The temptation of which the whole Bible speaks does not have to do with the testing of my strength, for it is of the very essence of temptation in the Bible that all my strength—to my horror, and without my being able to do anything about it—is turned against me; really all my powers, including my good and pious powers, fall into the hands of the enemy power and are now led into the field against me. Before there can be any testing of my powers, I have been robbed of them.
>
> This is the decisive fact in the temptation of the Christian, that he is abandoned, abandoned by all his powers—indeed, attacked by them—abandoned by all men, abandoned by God himself. His heart shakes, and has fallen into complete darkness. He himself is nothing. The enemy is everything. God has taken his hand away from him. "He has left him for

a little while" (Is 54:7). The man is alone in his temptation. Nothing stands by him. For a little while the devil has room. The hardest and highest temptation and suffering that God sometimes attacks and exercises his greatest saints with is when the heart of man feels nothing less than that God has abandoned him with his grace.[9]

Having a bit of trouble because the best things about you have betrayed the best things about you? Has the truth you've been telling upset people so much that they've resorted to character assassination to get you to shut up? Feeling like God moved and forgot to leave you a forwarding address? If all your strengths have been turned against you and God seems to be deaf to your cries, take courage. You are at the place of "broken bread and spilled out wine," that special seat at the table of forgiveness where God allows you to pour out the essential nature of who you are so that you can learn how to live out of the essence of who you truly are called to be—no matter what.

No matter what others tell you about yourself. No matter what the circumstances of your situation tell you about yourself. No matter what your own inner doubts and fears tell you about yourself.

The place of broken bread and spilled out wine is where you learn that no matter how many roaring, hungry lions are walking around you, the Bread of Life lives within you and He's a big enough loaf to feed you and everyone who wants to devour you—no matter what.

The Final Exam

So, here's the real test of the school of abandonment: what will you do, who will you be, in the midst of your abandonment? While Joseph was stepping around camel dung on his way to the Egyptian slave block, he had to grapple with whether he was going to work for the well-being of his master or whether he was going to say, "You don't own me and you can't make me." When Potiphar's wife tried to seduce him, he had to decide whether he was going to give in and get some (after all, he was a red-blooded Jewish boy) or remember that loving your neighbor in ways that are real and true are more important than a few feel-good hours.

During those long prison nights, fellow inmates could have heard Joe mumbling to himself, "Let 'em rot! They deserve it!" Then, they might have heard him flop over on that hard slab of wood he called a bed and whisper, "But if I treat them like they've treated me, I lose myself. God, if you're up there anywhere, help me!"

Finally, years later, when his brothers came begging bread, Joseph looked long and hard into their eyes and wondered, "Do I feed them to the sharks, or do I invite them to the banqueting table?"

In the Garden of Gethsemane, Jesus pounded the ground as He grappled with whether He was going to keep the Bread of Life to Himself or allow it to be broken to feed the world. Later, when Peter cut the ear off a soldier who'd come to arrest Jesus, He held the torn flesh in His hand for a split second, weighing whether He should let the one who'd come to kill Him bleed or be an agent of healing for someone who didn't want to hear His truth. As He hung on the cross, Jesus had to decide whether He was going to merely sink into His own pain or reach beyond it to embrace the thief hanging beside Him and comfort the mother who never quite seemed to grasp His mission.

When we are abandoned by others, when we feel abandoned by God, the temptation is to abandon our highest and best self. We get confused about who we really are. Asking ourselves over and over, "What did I do wrong and when did I do it and who am I because I did it?" we fall into the "who" and "what" of the endless navel-gazing of introspection.

Often, we are helped along here by the taunts of those standing near the foot of our cross. If you think introspection is an important part of forgiveness, you're right: We do have to shake the dirt out of our own laundry before we can help our brother wash his. But beware of the overuse of introspection; its confusion drains off the energy to love. As long as we're all absorbed in what's wrong with us, all of our energies go into the defense budget. We're just too tired and too consumed with pain to give anything to anybody. We'll talk more about that in the next chapter.

If you find that your struggle to forgive has enrolled you in the night school of abandonment, where all that is best in you temporarily conspires against all that is best in you, break bread with Joseph and Jesus and all the saints down through the ages who have lingered at this seat at the table of forgiveness. Let the lessons they learned there speak to you now.

Do not be afraid to eat the bread of abandonment. Do not fear when the wine of self has been spilled out—it is the last stage before stepping into the richness of life. For it is only as you are broken bread and spilled out wine that you learn how to let go of all the noise and distractions which masquerade as life and hold fast to that which gives true life: being who He created you to be, the very image of the Bread of Life and the Cup of Strong Wine in a world that hungers and thirsts for that which satisfies. The wheat for this bread is planted with tears, raised with tears, and baked with tears, and it breaks your teeth as you chew it. The grapes for this wine are crushed under many feet and taste most bitter going down. But, once they reach your belly, they bring sweet life to your soul and become an everlasting feast for others.

Thinking It Through

1. Bonhoeffer said, "This is the decisive fact in the temptation of the Christian, that he is abandoned, abandoned by all his powers—indeed, attacked by them...." Which of your strengths has become a weakness? How did it occur, and in what ways did your strength effectively undermine your ability to get out of the situation? How did you forgive yourself?

2. Remember a situation in which you experienced a killing abandonment. What was trapped inside of you? What did you wish could emerge? How did you forgive those who abandoned you? What happened to your spiritual life during this time—were you able to stay plugged in? If so, how?

3. Jesus didn't just feel abandoned, He *was* abandoned. How is it good bread for you to know that Jesus experienced a killing abandonment?

TWELVE

Got Bread?

Justified maltreatment can have more devastating human consequences than acknowledged cruelty.... When blame is convincingly ascribed, victims may eventually come to believe the degrading characterizations they hear about themselves.[1]

Albert Bandura

The reverent fear and worshipful awe of the Lord includes the hatred of evil; pride, arrogance, the evil way, and perverted and twisted speech I hate.

PROVERBS 8:13, AMPLIFIED

For several years, our daughter was a member of Pony Club. The day before events, the young people would ride or trailer their horses over to the club. As each horse arrived, it was put into a pasture with all the other horses. The first few times all the horses were together, they had to be watched pretty closely. That's because the horses were busy biting and kicking each other so they could establish their pecking order.[2]

The rule among horses is whoever bites the hardest and kicks the longest moves to the top of the pecking order. Those who don't bite very hard or kick very long move to the bottom of the ladder. Once the order is established, things settle down pretty well—unless one of the horses decides he wants to move up in the pecking order. Then the superior horses have to remind the little twerp of his place.

Chickens and dogs do the same thing; they peck and bite and growl their way to the top. We had Rhode Island Red laying hens for a number of years. It was Christmas every morning as I'd take my egg basket down to the barn and gather fresh eggs for breakfast. I would ooh and ahh over each offering, and I loved to stroke their soft feathers as I thanked them for the omelet we were about to enjoy. But it always hurt me to see the hens that were at the bottom of the pecking order. They'd had their feathers pulled out, and they were so submissive when I stroked them.

The roosters were the worst. One summer we acquired some roosters because we had this idealistic notion that we'd like to wake up to cock-a-doodle-doo. The roosters would indeed greet the morning sun with a great cacophony of crowing—but they had a dark side. They'd strut around the barnyard pecking and flying at each other and being quite vicious to the hens. The poor hens would be innocently digging for grubs and the roosters would come up and attack them, just to remind them who was in charge. Finally, one day I saw a rooster really do a job on a hen, and I said, "That's it. You guys are soup." We never had another Rhode Island Red rooster.

Learning the Tribal Customs[3]

In this world's system, whoever bites the hardest and kicks the longest is top dog. I don't know if you've noticed it, but when you walk into a roomful of people, a pecking order is in the process of being established. It's accomplished through subtle put-downs and bragging rights, which are a bit more socially acceptable than kicking and biting, but which feel every bit as wounding to your spirit. The goal is to convince you that you are less worthy than the other person so you won't challenge his or her authority.

Men do this through bragging about their accomplishments, their cars, their latest toy, their sexual conquests, or where their kids went to school; by name-dropping, talking about how much they have in their 401K, or hinting about the deals they have cooking. Women do this by talking about their clothes, their children's achievements, where they went on vacation, what clubs they belong to, who they know, their husband's job, their dress or bust size, and how they manage to keep their homes so well. If they're professional women, they can employ the same tactics the men use, referring to their professional achievements. This is especially effective when they are relating to women who are homemakers, who know right away that they couldn't possibly be as bright or as capable as a woman who is a CEO of a company.

Both men and women are equal-opportunity offenders when it comes to put-downs such as "Oh, really," or "Well, that will never work," or "What a dumb idea," or "You always have to be right," or "Did anyone ask you?" or "Get off my back."

Christians have their own ways of kicking and biting each other such as "You shouldn't feel like that" or "What would Jesus think about what you just did?" or "Scripture says..." or "You just need to submit and trust God to work out the details" or any of a host of ways we marginalize others' fears, needs, and concerns.

Usually, put-downs come not so much from what others say as from their subtle body language—such as interrupting us, looking around while we're talking, stepping in front of us in line, crossing their arms, smirking, rolling their eyes, shaking their heads, not looking at us when we speak, or not responding to our statements. These signals imply we don't deserve to take up the same air space. Often, we don't register these put-downs on a conscious level, but deep inside, we know we've been told to move to the back of the line.

Kicking and biting has been around since the earth's crust hardened. Adam tried it with God when he was confronted about eating the fruit from the Tree of the Knowledge of Good and Evil. "The woman *you* gave me caused all this trouble." Translation: "How can you question what I've done? I don't have to answer to anyone anymore, because eating this fruit made me just like You. I don't have to be under You in the pecking order anymore; that's what the serpent promised. Anyway, if this thing turned out all wrong, it's all Your fault because You gave me this woman and she gave me the fruit. So get off my back, God."

The scribes and Pharisees regularly tried it with Jesus, because once they saw all He had to offer, they were afraid they'd lose their place in the pecking order. So they followed Him around, then told Him He was doing things wrong (bite), asked Him who He thought He was (kick), accused Him of the very things they were guilty of (bite, bite), and generally acted as if they had the right to barge in and take over His day (kick, kick). Jesus didn't give in to the kicks and bites, and His noncompliance infuriated the religious leaders of His day, who kicked and bit Him all the way to Calvary.

The disciples were into carving out their place in the pecking order, too. "Jesus, we told those upstarts to stop teaching others about You because they aren't part of our elite group" (kick). "Jesus, who's going to be greatest in Your Kingdom?" (bite). "Jesus, who's going to get to sit at Your right hand?" (kick). "Jesus, can we call fire down from heaven and toast those who aren't cooperating? Huh, Jesus, can we, can we?" (kick, kick, bite, bite).

Unfortunately, not much has changed in the last 2,000 years. When *An Affair of the Mind* came out, I started traveling and meeting some pretty well-known Christian leaders. After being with some of them, I would come away feeling energized, but after being with others, I would come away feeling pummeled. It took me a long time to figure out what the difference was.

Finally, the light came on after I met one man who, no kidding, right after I introduced myself, told me how many houses he owned. In the next sentence, he told me about all the great ministry opportunities coming his way. Clearly, I was not anywhere near his place on the food chain. Imagine my horror when, some time later, I met someone and immediately told him about all the great ministry opportunities coming my way. I was learning how to play the game and it sickened me.

Home Sweet Pecking Order

In our homes the pecking order is often established by kicking and biting. Parents marginalize children, children disrespect parents, husbands cut down wives, wives put down husbands. This is especially true when secret sin is involved. I see it all the time as I talk to family members of pornography users. Pornography objectifies people. In order to use someone up for your own pleasure, that person needs to be beneath you on the food chain. So you need to use many kicking and biting techniques to keep your underdog in line. Because, if for one moment you allow yourself the realization that what you have before you is a living, breathing, human soul with hopes and dreams and gifts and songs to sing, you can't consume at will.

One of the ways evil facilitates its cannibalization of others is through lying. Of the many hundreds of letters I have in my files, in every single case deception was practiced as part of pornography usage. Those using porn first lie to themselves about how their value systems are changing and about the way they're consuming others to feed their own inner hungers. Then they lie to their spouses. The wife puts the kids to bed by herself after her husband tells her he has to work late—but what he's really doing is downloading teen porn off the Internet. The wife is holding down the home front while hubby is out of town on business, but he accidentally forgets to mention the strip club or the escort service or the in-room pornographic video that's part of this week's business trip. Or maybe he accidentally forgets to mention the many thousands of dollars accruing interest on a charge card his wife doesn't know he has because most of the charges come from the sex-for-hire trade.

Deceit is abusive. Deceit says that you don't deserve to know things that are essential to your health and happiness. Deceit believes that if you knew the whole truth, you wouldn't let the deceiver have what he or she wants. If you are practicing deception, you must of necessity keep others in your family disempowered. You must keep them in a constant state of confusion about what is really going on, and every time they get close to the truth, you must kick and bite.

A deceiver uses mind games, insisting you don't know what you're talking about or asking why you think you need to know that or maybe even torquing your sense of fair play. One woman wrote that when she questioned her husband about his porn usage, he cried and said over and over, "I can't believe you think I'd do such a thing. How can you be so cruel to me?" He portrayed her as a mean person for even suggesting such a thing. In the end, he got quite a lot of sympathy from others, who told her she was domineering and not submissive and offending God by not trusting her husband. She almost went insane trying to figure out the truth.

In another case, a husband manhandled his wife. She called the police and filed charges. The woman's church was not happy that she had resorted to the "secular authorities" for help. After all, didn't Paul counsel that we should avoid going outside the church for justice? Problems like this should be kept in the church and dealt with by the elders of the church, she was advised. The only hitch was the church's reluctance to judge the manhandling as a violation of the marriage covenant. Instead, this woman was asked what she had done to provoke it.

When one wife discovered that her husband was guilty of multiple adulteries, she wanted a separation (not a divorce). The leaders of her church told her that they would not give their permission for a separation. They said that if she separated from her husband, he would probably continue sinning and then the church would have to excommunicate him. Thus, to avoid putting his soul in mortal danger, she should stay with him and examine where she had failed as a wife.

The charges of being "domineering," "unsubmissive," and "not trusting" seem to be the favorite kicks and bites directed toward Christian women who are coping with betrayal in their marriages. Most of the letters I get tell the same sad story. These kicks and bites from husbands, family members, and church leaders are marvelously effective, because the last thing a woman who really loves God wants to do is challenge authority. Often, the next statement in the letter is that once duly kicked and bitten, the woman tried to follow the advice and to submit to the craziness. Invariably, she ended up either suicidal or feeling as if she was going crazy herself.

Herein lies one myth of "codependence." These women usually started out healthy. They tried very hard to figure out what was really going on, so they could deal with the realities in their lives. They didn't go into denial. But through the evasion of their husbands and the cruel naiveté of their church leaders, they were stripped of the truth and the strength to act on it. Then, when these same women walked into a counseling office years later, they were told they were "codependent enablers." See, in the kicking and biting business, you just keep moving to the back of the line.

Pardon Me While I Disembowel Myself

This morning, I received a letter from a woman who was told that the ideal Christian wife should do this and the ideal Christian wife should do that. She was told that she was a role, not a person. She was told that if she played her role right, her husband would sit at the gates of the city. Implied in this was that if her husband *wasn't* sitting at the gates of the city, it must be her fault. She was shamed into taking on more and more responsibility for the well-being of her family with little corresponding authority, because she was also told that she had to somehow be weaker than her husband, who was very passive.

If she had been given the authority to shoulder all this responsibility, she would have moved higher in the pecking order, something her husband refused to allow since that might make her less compliant. Her church leadership could not allow it either because it would challenge their understanding of "submission."

In the meantime, her husband, who was dealing with a full plate of guilt, regularly bit her with his abusive tongue and kicked her with pushes and shoves. When she tried to get some help for this abuse, she was charged by her church leadership with being "too strong." After that, when she tried to guide her children and run her house, she was always afraid of being charged with taking things into her own hands. So she ended up chasing herself in circles, working herself into horrendous exhaustion, and feeling terribly guilty for the accompanying "psychological problems" like loss of patience and depression. She spent days in bed just trying to regain her strength, all the while crying and wondering why submission wouldn't fix the problems in her home. She ended up suicidal, burned-out, and wanting to let it all go.

Killing Me Not So Softly With Your Words

Not long ago, I cleaned out my freezer. I hadn't opened it for several years, and the contents were so telling about what had happened to my heart. There, in various stages of freezer burn, were meals and baked goods dated six years previous. There were no packages with later dates. As I took the packages out, I realized that the last year I had "cooked ahead" was the year Steve and I separated due to his addiction to pornography.

When I went to get help shortly after Steve's confession about his involvement with pornography, a pastor told me Steve needed to learn to stand up to me. He told me Steve was so weak because I was so strong, that Steve wouldn't need to lie to me if I weren't so demanding. At the time, Steve was meeting with this pastor weekly and lying to him. I fled the office crying so hard the snot was running down my face. At that point, my heart died.

Years earlier, a pastor I had talked with about our marriage problems had applied John the Baptist's words about the coming of the Messiah to the husband-wife relationship. "He must increase, so you must decrease," he told me. "If he is weak in an area, you must be weaker," he insisted. I was told if I would do this, then Steve would become the man God always intended for him to be.

At that time, it never occurred to me that this man was taking the verse in John 3:30 way out of context. John the Baptist was simply commenting on the fact that his ministry was only the appetizer for the banquet God was about to set for the world in His Son. When the banquet is served, people stop eating the appetizers. Besides, Jesus never told His followers to decrease so He could increase. Instead, He told them that they would do greater works than He did (Jn 14:12). Because I failed to see the error here, I thought God required me to decrease so Steve could increase.

That misbelief started me on a tortuous struggle to figure out how to manage my home and love my children and still be weaker than Steve, who at that time was very passive because all his energy was going into his secret addiction. All my strengths had been turned against me. Not one of them could help me because, after all, they were "what was wrong with my marriage." Meanwhile, I was getting more and more exhausted. The fear of being too strong had already caused severe personality distortions and greatly impacted my ability to mother. Now here I was, all these years down the road, being given the same advice again. I hadn't killed myself enough, I was told.

As I threw the freezer-burnt packages into the trash, I thought back to the days before I'd gone for "help." I thought about how the first cold day of autumn, I'd go out and buy twenty-five or thirty pounds of chicken, simmer it all night on our wood stove, and in the morning pack gallons and gallons of rich golden stock into plastic containers and store them in the freezer until they could be made into soups and chicken pot pies, both for us and for friends and neighbors who might need a meal brought in. I chuckled, remembering the family joke that Mom's chicken soup could cure anything—and then I grimaced as I tried to remember how many years it had been since I'd put any stock in the freezer.

I thought about all the pies and casseroles I'd put in that freezer and all the quarts of applesauce and pints of jams and fruit butters I'd canned every fall. I'd been so happy to provide for my family that way. It never, ever seemed like drudgery, because I kept their faces in my heart as I worked and thought about how very much they would enjoy these treats in the days ahead. I thought about how many times in the years since then the apples had rotted in the orchard, how many times I'd contemplated getting chickens again or planting a garden but just couldn't bear to do it. Chickens and gardens plunged me into despair over shattered dreams and into confusion over what it meant to manage my home in a way that was weaker than Steve's weakness.

I thought about the loving notes I used to leave on my children's pillows and tuck into Steve's lunches. I thought about how my heart would sing as I cleaned my home because I was making a welcoming place for the ones I loved the most. I thought about how patient I had been with my children and how gentle I'd been with other people. I thought about how I used to love to sew curtains for my windows and clothes for my children and about the pride I'd felt when I knew my children were warmly dressed and my home beautifully decorated with things I had created for them. I thought about how long it had been since I had done these lovely, loving things or found any joy in being a wife or mother. I thought about how very feminine I'd been at one time and the ways I'd masked that femininity because my womanly heart was told to die.

Humility: Occupying Your Place With Grace

An incorrect understanding of submission can lead you to think that the wife must have either no power or very limited power so the husband can have all the power or most of the power. This is not a loving relationship, this is an abusive relationship. In healthy relationships, each person has a sense of personal power. We read in 2 Timothy 1:7, "For God hath not given us a spirit of fear; but of power and of love and of a sound mind." This verse makes it clear that a sense of personal power precedes love and leads to a sound mind. Without a sense of personal power, we are condemned to live in fear. Interestingly, women whose incorrect understanding of submission requires them to be powerless live in a constant state of generalized anxiety.

In her book, *The Verbally Abusive Relationship,* Patricia Evans says personal power comes from being connected to your feelings and it increases your sense of inner security, purpose, and meaning. When you have a sense of personal power, you are able to operate on the basis of loving mutuality. In loving mutuality, spouses value and celebrate each other's gifts as well as understand and honor each other's zones of authority.

[In loving mutuality,] "each person realizes that:
To bring one's thoughts and to hear the other's,
To express one's enthusiasm and to delight in the other's,
To reveal one's self and to reflect the other,
To value one's self and to esteem the other,
To enjoy one's creations and to treasure the other's,
To pursue one's growth and to nurture the other's,
To cherish one's solitude and to honor the other's,
To follow one's interests and to encourage the other's,
To act at one's pace and to accept the other's,
To indulge one's self and to give to the other,
To involve one's self and to assist the other,
To protect one's self and to comfort the other,
To see one's self and to behold the other,
To be one's self and to let the other be,
   Is to love one's self and to love the other."[4]

This is the mutual submission described in Ephesians 5:21-33. We are to submit ourselves one to another in the fear of God, wives submitting to their own husbands as unto the Lord and husbands loving their wives as Christ loved the church and gave Himself for her. Because, Paul tells us, the great mystery of marriage is a picture of the relationship between Christ and His church. It is important to note that Christ gives His bride the power and authority necessary to fulfill her purpose. Just before He ascended into Heaven, Christ urged the disciples to tarry in Jerusalem until they received the promise of the Father, "But ye shall receive power, after that the Holy Ghost is come upon you: and ye shall be witnesses unto me both in Jerusalem, and in all Judea and in Samaria, and unto the uttermost parts of the earth.[5]

When we have a sense of personal power, we don't have to seize our place, we simply have to occupy it. And we occupy it to serve one another with grace. "Let this mind be in you, which was also in Christ Jesus, who being in the form of God, thought it not robbery to be equal with God: But made Himself of no reputation and took upon Him the form of a servant."[6]

Understanding personal power is crucial if your spouse is involved in pornography. If someone is involved with pornography all their relationships will begin to change. In pornography, the primary relationship is with people who have been objectified for the viewer's pleasure, so those who use it start to see others as one-dimensional objects they can manipulate for their own pleasure.

When you have been objectified, you are treated with indifference, criticism, disregard and rejection. Objectification is abusive and it is killing to your spirit. Deep feelings of sadness accompany objectification. These feelings are most commonly recognized as "a sick feeling in the pit of my stomach," "an ache in my throat," or "a stab in my heart."[7]

In recent years, there has been much discussion in the church about protecting the traditional family. If we are going to truly advocate for the family, we must be clear that behaviors which objectify or abuse others are completely unacceptable. We must not rename these behaviors as "low self-esteem." We must not blame the victim of these behaviors for not being submissive enough. And we must begin to listen to each other. If the traditional family is functioning in a healthy way, it is the most wonderful place to be and we will naturally seek it. If the traditional family is functioning in an unhealthy way, it can be hell on earth and we will naturally flee it and no amount of pontificating will change our minds.

No Trespassing

One way to overcome evil is through choosing to do good. Therefore, evil's nefarious plan, through accusation and objectification, is to seek to destroy our sense of personal goodness and personal choice. Paul said,

> Repay no one evil for evil, but take thought for what is honest and proper and noble—aiming to be above reproach in the sight of everyone.... Beloved, never avenge yourselves, but leave the way open for God's wrath; for it is written, Vengeance is Mine, I will repay, says the Lord. But if your enemy is hungry, feed him; if he is thirsty, give him drink; for by so doing you will heap burning coals upon his head. Do not let yourself be overcome by evil, but overcome evil with good.[8]

These verses tell us we can make choices about how we will respond to evil. But in order to make choices, we have to have a sense of personal power, which is why evil seeks to break our will and destroy our strength. Through repeated accusation and objectification, evil attempts to turn us into victims by rendering us hopeless. After a while, we no longer believe that our choices will make any difference in the quality of our lives. Once we believe this lie, hope dies and our will is broken.

For this reason, an essential part of forgiveness is regaining both our place and our person. When someone sins against us, he or she trespasses on our property or on our person. In a sense that person tries to take our place in the scheme of things and treat it as if it was his or her own. This is especially true in sexual sin where the one involved in the adultery essentially invites someone else to take the place that only the spouse is legally allowed to occupy.

In addition to supplanting their spouses, those involved in sexual sin also attempt to rob their spouses of their personhood by objectifying them. If you are giving your body to another woman, it is not possible to look your wife in the eye and tell her you love her without first rendering her soulless. You must paint her as black as possible in your mind to offset your own guilt. You must shut your ears to her cries.

After she heard this concept, one woman said, "Something really strong and dignified began to rise up within me, and I said to myself and to Don that I *am* his wife and I will occupy every inch of that territory. I said that I am a person and I will not retreat from my personhood. He may be afraid of intimacy and he may be afraid to look at all that I am, but I am and I will be. I will set the table and I will offer bread and I won't back down.

"I began to see Don differently, too. So many times over the years, he's portrayed himself as a victim, too frightened to do what's right. His weaknesses have been his excuses for not doing what's right. I began to see him not as weak but as very capable. I began to see that it wasn't fear but contempt that governed his choices. I don't mean that fear isn't part of what drives him, but you can be afraid and still treat other people with respect. His meanness was an indication of contempt, not fear.

"I told him so and he denied it, but then God, with His infinite sense of humor, prompted someone at work to talk to Don and tell him that he was really sarcastic. He had other people tell him that he has an attitude. When he told his counselor what was going on, his counselor asked him to describe his behaviors and then told him those behaviors were abusive.

"This is all very hard for a man who's always wanted everyone to believe he's a really nice guy. But he's starting to see it, even to the point of telling his parents and sister that he's been abusive. Now he carries a list around of the things that are important to me, and he's actually working on them."

THE READER: "Hold it for a second. Do you mean there's something going on that's more important than my getting what I want?"

LAURIE: "Yes—something much more important. God is in the business of bringing about not just what you want but who you are."

THE READER: "What do you mean, 'who I am'?"

LAURIE: "You know that Romans 8:28 passage about how all things work together for good according to His purpose? Well, the next verse tells us what that purpose is: 'For those whom He foreknew—of whom He was aware and loved beforehand—He also destined from the beginning to be molded into the image of His Son and share inwardly His likeness, that He might become the firstborn among many brethren'" (AMPLIFIED).

THE READER: "So His purpose is that I be conformed to the image of His Son. That reminds me of that passage in Genesis that says, 'God said, Let Us make mankind in Our image, after Our likeness....'"

LAURIE: "Doesn't that blow you away? God created us in His *own* image and likeness. That image was marred when sin entered into the world and the firsthand knowledge of God and what life was like before the Fall was gradually lost."

THE READER: "And I think Adam and Eve knew just how far they had fallen because they saw 'before and after.' They knew from experience not only what it's like to walk and talk with God face-to-face but also the full purpose for which we've been created. They could tell their children 'back in the good old days' stories."

LAURIE: "So you're saying we start life at a disadvantage because we enter the world pretty clueless about who we were really created to be. It's like being given the pieces of a jigsaw puzzle without being given the cover of the box so we can see what the thing is supposed to look like when we get it all together."

THE READER: "Forgiveness must have a lot to do with getting a peek at that box top because when we're forgiving, we have to spend a lot of time gazing on Jesus."

LAURIE: "Yes, and as we gaze at Jesus we begin to understand how it is possible to choose to do good, because He teaches us what God looks like with skin on. We also come to understand that if we are the temple of His Holy Spirit and if we are a habitation of God, all that is good has come to dwell in us."

A Spittin' Image

In the Garden of Eden, God created man in His own image. In the womb of Mary, God created Himself in man's image. In forgiveness, God re-creates man in the image of His Son. "Behold, what manner of love the Father hath bestowed upon us, that we should be called the sons of God.... Beloved, now are we the sons of God, and it doth not yet appear what we shall be: but we know that, when He shall appear, we shall be like Him; for we shall see Him as He is."[9]

That word *see* is the Greek word *optomai*. It means to perceive with the eyes, and implies much more than the mere act of seeing. *Optomai* implies that we actually perceive, contemplate, experience, attain, and enjoy what we're seeing.

Seeing God in such a way transforms us. How we see God has everything to do with whether we can be salt to the perishing and light to the darkness. How we define Him has everything to do with whether we can find the courage to take back our place and our person.

The New Ager says, "When I see myself, I see God." He gets his definition of God from his definition of himself. The victim says, "When I see others, I see God." He derives his definition of himself from the way others define him.

But the Christian says, "When I see God, I see myself." A Christian defines himself based on his definition of God. For this reason, it is essential that we see Him as He really is. Any incorrect understanding about God will become incorrect understanding about ourselves.

"And every man that hath this hope in him purifieth himself, even as he is pure."[10]

Serious Bread

The Old Testament prophets saw God as external to themselves. He came and visited them from time to time, and He sent His Spirit to rest upon them. But in our day, God has done a new thing. He now dwells within us. The Ark of the Covenant has been moved from a gold-encrusted box of acacia wood into the innermost parts of our hearts. He has written His law on our hearts. He has given us His rod to rule and reign with Him, and daily He meets with us over the mercy seat and feeds us the bread of His love. And this makes all the difference, because now the power to define our place in the scheme of things is not external, it's internal.

Think of Peter out there walking on the water in the middle of the night. When he saw Jesus coming toward his boat, his heart leapt with the possibility of belief. Maybe all that he had seen Jesus do, he could do, too. So he climbed out of the boat and walked onto the waves. We're talking waves, big waves, great BIG waves. He was doing fine as long as he could see Jesus, but when a wave came out of nowhere and hid Jesus from his sight, Peter panicked. He lost hope and he started to sink.

For Peter, at that time, Christ was external. He could be lost to sight. But now He is in us and He can never, ever be lost. "Christ in you the hope of glory."[11] The hope that I can reflect the wholeness of who I was created to be, no matter what. That is the one thing evil can't take from you, although it will lie to you about it forever and will try to convince you to lie to yourself about it.

He is our Emmanuel. The God who is with us and in us and for us and to us and through us. Nothing, absolutely nothing, not the death of our hopes, nor the failures in our lives, nor our fears about the future, nor our doubts about the past, nor the pile of guilt we can't quite dig out of, nor the load of shame we so desperately try to shake off, nor anything else that has ever happened to us or ever will happen to us can separate us from the love of God which is in Christ Jesus our Lord.

I lived most of my life looking for that pinprick of light that let me know the way out of the darkness. Then, one day, I realized the Light of the World lives within me and it doesn't matter how dark it is out there—I carry the Light wherever I go. I don't have to look for the way out anymore, because the Way Out lives within.

The kicks and bites of evil no longer define me, although I show a bruise now and then. Instead, I am learning to listen with a disciple's ear to what my God says: "I no longer call you servants, I call you friends."[12] "Everything that the Father has is Mine. That is what I meant when I said that He will take the things that are Mine and will reveal, declare, disclose and transmit them to you."[13]

When we stop trying to be good and rest in His goodness in us, we're talking serious bread.

Thinking It Through

1. Had any good kicks and bites lately? How does the group you hang around with establish a pecking order? How do you view pecking order?

2. How is the pecking order set in your church? What happens to people who are six fries short of a full Happy Meal when it comes to your church's expectations? How is the pecking order brought about in your home? What are the effects of this way of telling who is top dog?

3. In what ways have you disemboweled yourself in response to the kicks and bites of others?

4. How does your view of God define how you see yourself?

THIRTEEN

Abigail's Legacy

The only feelings that do not change are those that are ignored. Pain has a size and a shape, a beginning and an end. It takes over only when not allowed its voice.[1]

Ann Brener

When I kept silence, my bones waxed old through my roaring all the day long.

PSALM 32:3

A while back, I heard a popular speaker counsel women against the danger of "taking things into their own hands." He cited the example of Abigail, wife of the fool Nabal.[2] Nabal was a wealthy man. He had 3,000 sheep and 1,000 goats.

One day, when David was hungry, he sent ten of his followers to ask Nabal if he would kindly give them something to compensate them for watching over his shepherds when they were in Carmel. Nabal's answer? "Buzz off."

Being a bit of a hothead himself, David responded, "He's toast. Guys, get your swords."

When Abigail found out that 400 guys with an attitude were headed toward her house, she boxed up 200 loaves of bread, two skins of wine, five barbecued sheep, five measures of parched grain, 100 clusters of raisins, and 200 cakes of figs and rode out to meet them. When she met David, she fell on her face in front of him and did obeisance. Then, kneeling at his feet, she said, "Please, don't make yourself into the same kind of fool my husband is. God has blessed you because you're a good man; don't let this insult provoke you to evil. If you go through with your plans to kill my husband, you'll never be able to forgive yourself."

David listened to her wise words and blessed her. When Abigail got home, her husband was drunk. After he sobered up the next morning, she told him what had happened. His "heart died within him," and he died ten days later. When David heard the news, he sent his servants to bring Abigail to him and later married her.

According to this speaker, when Abigail countermanded Nabal's orders by feeding David and his men, she took things into her own hands, and this is something women should avoid at all costs. This speaker believed that God judged Abigail for being too strong, and he equated strength in a woman with lack of submission. He encouraged women that even if they were living with men who were abusive and difficult, they should just trust the Lord to take care of whatever consequences might come their way.

This speaker totally overlooked the fact that Scripture says David blessed Abigail's discretion and advice. He was actually pleased because this strong woman didn't fit into his model of hierarchical authority, a model in which the people superior to you in the pecking order are to be obeyed no matter how evil or foolish their orders are. In addition to wrongly interpreting Scripture, this speaker offered women absolutely no hope that there was any way out of their predicaments except to disregard their own strengths and passively wait on God, expecting that somehow He would suspend the law of cause and effect for them. Jesus condemned that type of thinking as utter arrogance. When Satan tempted Him to defy the law of gravity and to throw Himself off the pinnacle of the Temple, He said, "It is written, you shall not tempt the Lord your God."[3]

The Bash Abigail Syndrome

This speaker was promulgating what I call the Bash Abigail Syndrome. I've seen many women devastated by this syndrome. Shamed by the judgment of others that they are unsubmissive or too strong, fearful that God will judge them for taking things into their own hands because they didn't trust Him enough, women affected by the Bash Abigail Syndrome become powerless to deal with the evil foolishness of their husbands. Their ability to mother is damaged, their ability to care for their home is devastated, their femininity is decimated, and their ability to truly love their husband is destroyed.

Rather than judging us for taking things into our own hands, God gave us hands because He intends for us to use them to take dominion.[4] For those who are hyperventilating over this thought, taking dominion is not the same thing as usurping a husband's authority. Taking dominion is using your strengths to walk in the authority necessary to fulfill the responsibilities God has given you.

God never asks us to do something without giving us the authority to do it. Because He asks women to do the incredibly challenging job of being keepers of their home, He gives them corresponding strength and authority. Proverbs 14:1 tells us a wise woman uses her strengths to build her house. Proverbs 31:17-18, 25 (AMPLIFIED) says of the virtuous woman,

> She girds herself with strength and makes her arms strong and firm. She tastes and sees that her gain from work is good; her lamp goes not out, but it burns on continually through the night of trouble, privation, or sorrow, warning away fear, doubt, and distrust.... Strength and dignity are her clothing and her position is strong and secure; she rejoices over the future, knowing that she and her family are in readiness for it.

When Abigail appealed to David for the life of her husband and the protection of her home, she was walking in the authority God gave her to keep her home. Her actions saved countless lives as well as preventing countless regrets for David. Those who tell a woman her strengths are to be cursed rob her of dignity and leave her with no way to handle the night of trouble, privations, and sorrow. They plunge her into fear, doubt, and distrust. The bread thief strikes again.

Beware though—just as in Abigail's case, whether you are a man or woman struggling to deal with a foolish spouse, the act of rising up and using your good bread to save your household may be the beginning of the end. Evil and foolishness do not easily retreat. They will kick and bite all the way. There are husbands and wives who, when they realize their spouses will no longer cower under their abuse, crank up their efforts to either shame or batter them into compliance. When their spouses continue to confront their cruel arrogance by offering the good bread of strength and dignity, some of these men and women will flee their families rather than change their behavior. But there are many other husbands and wives who, once they are confronted with good bread, will begin to turn from their arrogant foolishness and risk opening themselves to the love and intimacy their deeply shamed hearts so long for.

The House of Mirrors

In 1 Peter 3, wives are counseled to adapt themselves to husbands who are not obeying God so these men may be won over, not by nagging but by the powerful example of a life well lived. God calls wives to adapt to their husband's weaknesses not by twisting and distorting themselves in the areas in which their husbands are twisted and distorted, but by being fearless in doing what's right.[5]

The woman who calls the police when her husband is physically abusive, or refuses to have sex because he is engaging in behaviors that put her at risk for STDs, or begins to manage the family budget because her children lack essentials due to her husband's profligate spending of the family money, or refuses to cover for his lies or join in his games of manipulation and control, will pay dearly for her courage. This is why she needs to be fearless in doing what's right. I can tell you from personal experience, when you step up to the plate and do what's right, all hell breaks loose against you and all heaven rallies around you.

Finally, let me say something about living with someone who is disrespecting you either through deceit, objectification, or verbal abuse. Tremendous psychological confusion accompanies abusive behavior. This confusion is intensified by the fact that the abuser often works very hard to appear to be really nice when he or she is around others. So, the abused spouse constantly feels that what's happening behind closed doors must be a misunderstanding. He or she wonders why the spouse treats him or her like an enemy and works hard to convey, "I'm really your friend." The type of submission that requires a husband or wife to be powerless feeds an abuser's need for complete control. If you find yourself in a relationship where you are regularly undermined, trivialized, blamed, criticized, discounted, blocked, or diverted from gaining important information, subjected to abusive anger, or where you frequently experience the silent treatment, I highly recommend you read Patricia Evans book, *The Verbally Abusive Relationship*.

The woman is the glory or reflection of the man. When she reflects back a lack of health to her husband through an improper understanding of submission, the mirror—which could instead have shown him where he's not reflecting the image of God in his own life—becomes distorted. What God designed to be a life-giving reflection becomes instead an incredible house of mirrors where every reflection is just as distorted as the image it's reflecting. But if she reflects back health to him, he may begin to get it. It is a way of saying she believes in him and in their goodness together. As she courageously adapts to his offer of moldy bread, not by eating, which a faulty idea of submission would require her to do, but by putting out good bread so he can taste and see that life is good, she walks out a radical forgiveness that has the power to set the self-centered captive free.

The Booger in My Soul That Rots My Bread

In order to offer good bread, we have to break free of shame. Shame is a feeling that there is something very wrong with you. Shame goes beyond feeling that others are staring at your nakedness. It feels more like your skin has been peeled off and people are turning green at the sight of your internal organs.

When you feel ashamed, you feel unacceptable to others and you disown yourself. Part of disowning ourselves is being unaware of our feelings or being dishonest about how painful something really is. It was easier for me to say I was angry about Steve's involvement with porn than it was for me to say I felt horribly rejected and unworthy because he preferred a fantasy to the reality of life with me.

People who feel a lot of shame feel like they're different from others. They think that others can tell they're different just by looking at them. In order to feel like they fit in, shamed people work very hard at living up to whatever standard they are told will make them acceptable, only they never quite feel like they make it.

In her powerful Bible study, *Shame, Thief of Intimacy,* Marie Powers says, "Keith Miller expressed his feelings of not belonging when he wrote, 'It was as if other people had been given a secret manual about how to get along and be loved and at home in life and I hadn't got one.'"[6]

Shame is kind of like having a booger stuck on the end of your finger—you can't shake it off no matter how hard you try. When this booger lodges in your soul, it acts like Velcro, and pretty soon there's a heap of stuff attached to it, all sending you one message: "Honey, you ain't got no bread worth eating. So just move to the back of the line."

Shame is a popular way to manage others because it's so darn effective. Most people would rather walk barefoot across broken glass than be told they are unworthy of being loved. Most people are very reluctant to go against the flow of the crowd because they fear the shame attached to being different from others. Peer pressure is a form of shame-motivated behavior because it uses the opinions of others to keep us in line.

Unfortunately, there are some churches where sanctified peer pressure is used to "help" people conform to holiness. Even though these churches preach salvation by grace alone through faith alone in Christ alone, they hand their congregation an incredible list of do's and don'ts that define the perfect Christian. Even though these churches preach "judge not lest you be judged," their congregations thoroughly inspect one another to see who is failing to live up to the church's standards. While preaching about loving one another, they use shame to silence those who have different viewpoints.

A woman once asked me if there wasn't some good shame. She said she used shame to keep her children in line. She thought if they were afraid of how others would perceive them, they might not misbehave. And you know, that works—sometimes. Many of us fear exposure as a wrongdoer and subsequent rejection by the crowd, so we straighten up and fly right. But God knows our heart is in captivity to the fear of man. Shame is old-man motivation. Whenever you allow feelings of shame to control your choices, you are walking in your fallenness.

This is why the gospel of grace is so dangerous. If I am accepted by God completely apart from my works, then shame has no hold on me and I do not need man's approval. What then will keep me in line? Only love. Love is the motivation of a heart that's been set free from shame. And only a heart set free from shame can truly love, because only that kind of heart can give selflessly. A shamed heart must be constantly reassured that it is accepted, so it loves in order to be loved. And the object of its affections feels the constant drain of silent expectations.

Strip Search

Shame must come off before forgiveness can be given or received because forgiveness is a gift of love. Shame comes off only one way—through the law of the covenant also known as the Ten Commandments (they are listed at the end of this chapter). God gave Moses the Ten Commandments on Mount Sinai after He had set the children of Israel free from 400 years of slavery. When the Israelites arrived at the foot of Mount Sinai, they had just been set free from traumatic circumstances. In their slavery, they were not allowed personal boundaries. Their property could be taken at will. Their bodies could be taken at will. They had no right to an opinion that didn't mirror the opinion of their slave master. These people had been victimized for 400 years.

Being victimized can make you think like a victim. Victims feel like the center of control is outside themselves because that is what happened in their victimization—someone bigger and more powerful than they were did something to them that they were powerless to control. Like all victims, the Israelites had their sense of what was right and what was wrong terribly tweaked because the people with the whips defined right and wrong by what they allowed and disallowed. So God had to give the Israelites a new way to know what was right and what was wrong. He said, "Through signs and wonders I set your bodies free; now through my law I'm going to show you how to set your souls free. And this is important because if you can't learn how to be free on the inside, you won't be able to remain free on the outside."

The Israelites had been walking in the darkness of victimization. They needed a light to show them the way to freedom. Isaiah 2:3-5 tells us that the light of the Lord comes from the law. Without the law, we are walking in darkness and have no way to avoid harming ourselves or being harmed by others. This is because the law brings justice. When there is justice, people do not need to be afraid and they do not need to fight, because perpetrators are restrained and the weak are protected.

The foundations of a society crumble when God's law is ignored, for having certain access to justice is the only way people can live together safely. The law of the covenant tells us that our interests will be protected in our interactions with others. Therefore, we are willing to risk trusting others, and trust is the only healthy way people can conduct business and work together for common interests. When we feel our interests have been violated, the law provides a way for us to appeal to a higher authority than mere public opinion in determining whether we have been treated with dignity and respect. When the law is enforced, justice is executed and the oppressor's rod is broken. Without justice, there will always be oppression because man is sinful, and in his sinful state he desires to lord it over others. The law says it is not OK for the strong to oppress the weak. The law tells us all people have equal rights to honor, possession of property, safety of person, protection of their marriage covenant, respect for their gifts, and preservation of their reputation.

The Case of the Purloined Dumptruck

In covenantal relationships, authorities serve in a judicial capacity. They are there to protect the innocent. In the days before Israel had kings, if someone felt his rights had been trampled on, he would go to the judges and give his side of the story. The judges would then hear the other side of the story and make a determination about whether boundaries had been crossed. A godly judge would protect the fatherless and the widow from scoundrels as well as make sure lawless people were held accountable for boundary violations.

Let's visit a common scene in many homes where a misunderstanding of the purpose of authority in covenantal relationships sets one child up to be an abuser and another child up to be a victim. Little Jimmy comes crying to mommy that little Bobby is playing with his toy dumptruck. Mommy tells little Jimmy that he needs to learn to share. She might even say, "Well, you weren't playing with it, so why can't he?"

What has little Bobby learned? He has learned that he doesn't have to respect property rights. It is OK for him to just go in and take whatever he wants. Little Jimmy has learned that he is either going to have to fight for what's his or learn not to care about his possessions. These are not the kinds of lessons you want your children to learn. Bobby needs to learn to ask for permission before he uses someone else's things and Jimmy needs to be assured that there's a higher law than brute force. If children are not taught these things while they are young, the strong-willed child becomes more and more disrespectful of others and the more compliant child feels more and more like a victim.

What about toys that are jointly owned? In many families, there are "my toys" and "our toys." When our children were little, if Ian was playing with a toy that was a family toy and Sandy wanted to play with it, I would tell the two of them, "I'll set the buzzer for fifteen minutes and when it goes off Sandy can play with the toy for the next fifteen minutes." When you're a kid, fifteen minutes is an eternity. Often, by the time the buzzer went off, Ian was already done playing with the toy or Sandy wasn't interested anymore. But, she knew she was going to get her turn and Ian knew he was going to get his. Sometimes, I would be pleased to find them sharing the toy. When your boundaries are respected, sharing is an act of generosity rather than a result of coercion.

In case you think I'm overemphasizing the importance of teaching children to respect each other's rights, imagine Jim and Bob thirty years down the road. Jim calls the police to report Bob has stolen his truck. Would the police tell Jim he just needed to learn to share his truck? How do you think the police would respond if when they picked up Bob he told them, "But he wasn't driving the truck when I took it."

You Either "Is" or You "Isn't"

In legalistic churches, people set up lists of do's and don'ts, dividing people into those who obey the do's and don'ts and those who refuse or fail and are therefore probably not believers. These people use the law as a divider. The law was given to be a reconciler, not a divider. It tells us how to live in harmony with others, by calling us to remember where we have failed to love, and helping us understand how others have failed to love us.

The law is the only way shame can be off-loaded because shame is a feeling attached to missing the mark. The law tells us what the mark is by defining right and wrong. Using the law, we are able to make judgments about guilt or innocence. This is why the law of the Lord is perfect, restoring the soul, because the law either pronounces us innocent, thus freeing us from guilt and shame, or it pronounces us guilty, thus showing the way to freedom.

The law doesn't ask what you were thinking when you transgressed. The law doesn't ask what your victim was thinking or what your spouse was thinking. The law simply asks two questions: Is the act you are charged with a violation of the law? And did you in fact commit the act? If the answer to both questions is "yes," then you are guilty as charged. Extenuating circumstances are not taken into account in determining guilt, although circumstances may be considered in determining punishment. (This is called "mercy." This is why the tables of the law are in the Ark of the Covenant under the mercy seat.)

The law either vindicates us or convicts us. In forgiveness, it is essential that both options are truly available. If someone hasn't done something wrong, there is no need to forgive him. You might need to forbear him or understand him or just let him do things his own way, but you do not need to forgive him if he is not guilty of breaking the law.

It turns out the law lets you win the battle against shame no matter how your verdict is rendered. If you are innocent, the case is closed. If you are guilty, your guilt was covered at the cross. At the cross, God used the law to judge us all quite guilty of violating the law. Then He covered our guilt with His blood and our shame with His righteousness. God invites you to be reconciled to Him not on the basis of your futile efforts but on the basis of faith in His goodness, love, and deep passion to see you set free from all that binds you. And He whispers to your deeply shamed heart, "There is therefore no condemnation in Christ Jesus, who came into the world, not to judge the world but that the world through Him might be saved from its own judgment and find rest from its shame."[7]

Mutually Assured Destruction

One of the difficulties of forgiveness is that the evildoer knows the law better than his victim knows it. The law is written in our hearts, and when we violate it, it accuses us day and night until we make things right. In order to silence their accusing hearts, those who are guilty of sin have a policy of mutually assured destruction. They use the flaming fiery darts of accusations to drive back their accusers.

In Ephesians 6:16 we are told to "lift up over all the covering shield of saving faith, upon which you can quench all the flaming missiles of the wicked one" (AMPLIFIED). Paul was writing about spiritual warfare and comparing it to the type of warfare the Roman soldiers practiced. Here, he was referring to high-tech arrows that were filled with combustible material. These arrows burst into flame when they hit the target. The goal was to either fry the enemy or drive him out into the open where he could be slaughtered. Satan is the accuser of the brethren, and if you've ever been accused, you've probably experienced a burning sensation down deep in your soul where the fiery missile hit. That burning feeling is a sign that you've just been shamed.

An arrow is a short-range weapon. It can be used to either gain territory or to guard strongholds. Those seeking to devour others use the fiery missiles of accusation in both ways. They get close to your boundaries and try to shame you into compliance. Or they shoot off arrows of accusation, hoping to shame you into oblivion when you accidentally get too close to discovering their lair.

A young Texan I'll call Brent Higgins stumbled too close to the lair of a liar and found a hail of arrows coming his way. On a Saturday afternoon in January of 1999, young Brent was driving around Midland, Texas, with a friend when they saw Midland High School principal Frank Diamond's (not his real name) car parked in front of a high school teacher's home. The married principal and the school teacher were nowhere to be seen. The friend snapped a picture of the empty car.

After developing the film, Higgins kept the picture in his closet. Although he never took the picture to school, the principal disciplined him for being disrespectful toward an adult by fostering rumors. Higgins said he didn't spread rumors, and according to thirty-five letters received by the school board in his defense, there had been rumors about the affair months before the picture was taken. When asked directly if the rumors were true, Diamond declined to answer.

When Higgins refused to write the apology that Diamond requested, "he was suspended for three days and placed in a school for students with behavior problems. He was also not allowed to attend his graduation."[8]

Blind the Eyes That Expose

What happened to young Brent Higgins is evil. The principal shamelessly tried to force him to make a false apology. Then, when that failed, he shamelessly condemned him to the gulag of problem-student education and further punished him by not allowing him to join his class at graduation. He did all of this out in the open, as if he were doing nothing wrong.

Evil cannot be shamed into compliance by fear of exposure because evil is shameless. But evil does seek to shame into oblivion those who would expose it. What is interesting about shame is that we can feel ashamed even if we are not guilty of any wrongdoing. This is the work of evil, because evil seeks to falsely accuse those who would expose it in order to silence their voices. Dan Allender says, "Shamelessness thrives on the ability to avoid exposure. A person can avoid the experience of shame if he can put out the eyes that see inside him. When his accuser is blind, he can escape the gaze that penetrates his soul. For that reason, evil almost always works to shame the other. Shame works to blind the eyes that expose."[9]

In her book *Is Nothing Sacred?*, Marie Fortune says, "Shooting the messenger is a common response to the revelation of unethical conduct. When the news is not something the institution or the community wants to hear, its knee-jerk reaction is to turn on the bearer of the news, often with a vengeance. First the messenger's credibility becomes the issue, and then her or his motivation is suspect. All of this serves to deflect the attention of the church from the real source of the problem ... and it relieves the church from doing anything about it."[10]

Fortune suggests that three main problems accompany the revelation of sexual sin: shooting the messenger, misnaming the problem, and blaming the victim.

"Each of these is an automatic, institutional response to the revelation of internal misjustice."[11] Each of these responses is a way evil shames the truth from a situation. And each of them will cut off the possibility of healing.

When we shoot the messenger, we pluck out our own eyes and plunge ourselves into the darkness of self-deception. When we misname the problem, such as calling sin low self-esteem, we cut off the possibility of repentance because we deliver the broken one from having to own his or her actions. When we blame the victimized spouse by focusing on what he or she has done to incur the abuse, we cut off the possibility of love and forgiveness because we have bound the wounded heart in shame.

Sadly, often in the church we are so afraid that caring about truth and seeking justice will lead to caring about vengeance and seeking punishment that we abandon truth and justice altogether.

Thinking It Through

1. Have you ever faced an enormously difficult challenge because your spouse failed to handle a situation correctly? How did you respond? What were the repercussions?

2. In what ways are you reflecting health to your spouse? In what ways are you distorting the image of real love? What misunderstandings about submission hinder your ability to offer your spouse "good bread"?

3. In what ways has shame been used to keep you in line? How do you use shame to keep others in line?

4. Since the law either pronounces you innocent or proclaims you guilty while offering the cross to cleanse your guilt, how can the law set you free from shame?

The Ten Commandments (from Ex 20:3-17)

Thou shalt have no other gods before me.
Thou shalt not make unto thee any graven image.
Thou shalt not take the name of the Lord thy God in vain.
Remember the Sabbath day, to keep it holy.
Honor thy father and thy mother.
Thou shalt not kill.

Thou shalt not commit adultery.
Thou shalt not steal.
Thou shalt not bear false witness against thy neighbor.
Thou shalt not covet.

FOURTEEN

When Paradigms Shift, Gears Grind

Sacred cows make the best hamburger.

Mark Twain

Whom do men say that I, the Son of Man, am?

Matthew 16:13

Are there any verses you would like to Exacto blade out of the Bible? I mean, just get in there and cut those buddies right out? There are passages I'm pretty sure the writers must have scribbled down when God was on vacation or something. Surely He couldn't mean I'm supposed to do *that!* My least favorite passage of all time, running only slightly ahead of some of Paul's writings in the unpopular vote, has been Matthew 5:38-42: "You have heard that it was said, An eye for an eye and a tooth for a tooth. But I say to you, Do not resist the evil man; but if anyone strikes you on the right jaw or cheek, turn to him the other one too. And if anyone wants to sue you and take your undershirt, let him have your coat also. And if anyone forces you to go one mile, go with him two miles" (Amplified).

This passage from the Sermon on the Mount poses serious problems for us forgivers. It looks like a setup for victimization. Take this situation, for instance. I just got off the phone with a pastor from another country. This pastor has a ministry that reaches around the world. He and his wife are greatly loved by their congregation. Everything looks so good on the surface. The pastor felt he could level with me since I had been so honest about my own struggles to understand what it means to love someone who presents one face to the world and another face to a spouse.

After twenty years of marriage, this pastor is ready to walk out. Their congregation would never guess, but since their honeymoon, this ideal Christian wife has been verbally abusing her husband.

She slices and dices him with her tongue for real and perceived failures. In public she is the adoring wife, but in private she tells him she doesn't care about him or his ministry. This is not just PMS or a bad hair day. This is not the reaction of a woman whose husband mistreats her. This is raw evil. This woman grew up in an abusive home and she hates men. When she looks at her husband there is a cold hardness in her eyes.

She regularly confuses him because she is able to stop her abuse on a dime. She can be screaming at him one minute and then sweet as pie the next. She does this most often when someone happens by. Then she becomes Mrs. Sociable, and he's left trying to scrape himself off the floor to say "hi."

He grew up in a loving home and brought a lot of stability into the marriage. He never guessed she was like this when they were dating because she very carefully kept her contempt hidden. Once her rage started, he naively thought all this woman needed was someone who loved her. So he turned the other cheek. He went the second mile. He did beautiful things for her. But his kindness only seemed to make her worse. He's fasted and prayed and prayed, but nothing has changed.

He's starting to lose his grip. He's never been unfaithful in thought or deed, but lately he's been struggling with thoughts of wanting to be with another woman. He's so frightened, knowing how much is at stake, but he can't seem to stop the thoughts. He said, "I'm just so lonely all the time."

He said he'd walk out tomorrow but he'd probably lose his ministry, because people who are divorced are the lepers of the Christian community. Then he paused and said, "I'd look like the bad guy because everyone loves Ellen so much. You know, the church loves you if you play by their rules, but if you start to become honest about what's going on in your life, they shut you right down." Should this pastor just passively continue to "turn the other cheek"? Should he continue to allow the battering of his soul and spirit, hoping that eventually "going the second mile" will plough up the hardness of his wife's heart?

Setting Yourself Up for Failure

A while back, I listened to the tearful confession of a pastor who did persevere in an impossible situation but ended up betraying himself and all that he holds dear by having sex with a woman he was counseling. He never, ever thought he would do something like that. He had a wife and two children whom he adored. His work as a pastor was very important to him, and he'd worked hard to make sure he ministered with integrity. His church was thriving, and he headed up a regional ministerial alliance.

Even though he knew it was wrong, he said he was thinking he'd really like to see this other woman again. "The sex was wonderful," he said. Then he spoke of the virtually nonexistent sex in his marriage. His wife was a victim of childhood sexual abuse. To her, sex equaled victimization. She told herself she'd been victimized enough and now that she was grown-up, she wasn't going to have sex anymore. "I understand her fears, but what am I supposed to do about my sexual needs?" he asked. He was afraid to tell her what had happened with this other woman for fear he'd lose his children. He was afraid to tell his board of elders what had happened for fear he'd lose his church. It seemed the only possible solution was to continue on in the misery. And he knew if he did that, he'd end up in bed with the other woman again. When his wife told him she didn't want to have sex anymore, did Jesus mean that this pastor should just deny his sexuality and hope for the best?

Moreover, we wonder if Jesus is telling us to allow others to take advantage of us as in this case: A man installed the plumbing on a new house for an elder in his church. When it came time to pay for the job, the elder paid only half the bill. The man waited to see if he would get the other half. After a year, he approached the elder and was told that he needed to honor those in authority over him. He then went to the elder board, where he was told that those in authority deserve double honor and he should just turn the other cheek in order to preserve the unity of the saints. So is Jesus telling this plumber that he should forget payment and give the elder his coat, too?

When Paradigms Shift, Gears Grind

No doubt about it, of all the verses I loved to hate, Matthew 5:38-42 was numero uno. That is, until I found Dennis, Sheila, and Matthew Linn's powerful book, *Don't Forgive Too Soon*. The Linns cite the award-winning book, *Engaging the Powers*, by Scripture scholar Walter Wink to explain that "Jesus' words probably mean the opposite of what we have usually thought. In Matthew 5:38-42 Jesus invites us to a forgiveness that, far from being passive and self-abusive, actively resists evil, maintains our dignity and invites the person who hurt us to recall his or her own dignity."[1]

So, let's take this passage apart bit by bit and see if we can't find courage from Jesus' words rather than a setup for victimization. Let's start with the troubling statement in verse 39a, "Do not resist the evil man."

Is Jesus saying we should roll over and play dead when evil comes against us?

If that's what He meant, He didn't take His own advice when He encountered evil in a Nazarene synagogue. As usual, Jesus entered the synagogue on the Sabbath. When it was time to read Scripture, Jesus stood up and unrolled the Isaiah scroll and read, "The Spirit of the Lord is upon me because the Lord has anointed me to preach the good news to the poor. He has sent Me to announce release to the captives, and recovery of sight to the blind; to send forth delivered those who are oppressed—who are downtrodden, bruised, crushed and broken down by calamity—To proclaim the accepted and acceptable year of the Lord—the day when salvation and the free favors of God profusely abound."[2]

Then, rolling up the scroll, Jesus sat down. Every eye was riveted on Him.

His voice rang out loud and clear: "Today, this Scripture has been fulfilled while you are present and hearing."

A hush fell over the crowd as the importance of the words sank into each heart. Then they began to whisper among themselves.

"Hey, Jacob, is this hometown boy the Messiah?"

"I don't know, Samuel. Isn't he Joseph's boy?"

"I think so. But I've heard he's been doing some pretty amazing stuff."

"Yeah, me too. Maybe he'll do something here."

Just when everyone was feeling really good about Him, Jesus did an "in your face."

"I know you guys are hoping I'll do some miracles here like I did in Capernaum. But I'm not going to," He said.

Enraged, the crowd jumped to their feet. Grabbing Him, they drove Him to the cliff at the edge of town, planning to throw Him off the precipice. Right when it looked like it was curtains, Jesus just passed through their midst and went on His way.

I don't know about you, but this passage makes me uncomfortable. If Jesus meant that we should just "take it" when evil comes against us, why would He have needlessly provoked evil into a confrontation? If Jesus meant we should allow the evil man to do whatever he wants to us, why would He have escaped the clutches of evil men and gone on?

Perhaps some of our difficulty comes from a faulty understanding of the word "resist." The Linns point out that the word we translate as "resist" in Greek means to "resist violently, to rise up in a military sense. Thus, Jesus is telling us not to take an eye for an eye, not to hit back or otherwise return violence in kind. Instead, when someone tries to abuse or humiliate us, Jesus invites us to find a creative, nonviolent way to resist and regain our dignity."[3]

The idea that there might be another way to handle conflict besides retaliation in kind (an eye for an eye) was totally new to this crowd. It was also something this group of people desperately needed because they were a captive people. Their Roman masters could abuse them at will, and if they fought back, they could be severely punished or killed. The very times they were living in required them to be creative in how they handled evil.

Sermon on the Mount, Take Two

Now that Jesus has the attention of His audience, He gives some examples of elegant ways to handle evil. In His first example, He says, "If someone comes up to you and strikes you on the right cheek, turn your left cheek to him." At first blush, this sounds like you're required to submit to battering. But Jesus' listeners would have heard it very differently because of their cultural customs.

In Jesus' day the right hand and the left hand had symbolic significance. When it came to giving and receiving, transactions were accomplished with the right hand only because the left hand was used for unclean purposes. Besides that, the Greeks believed that the left side was unlucky and an evil omen, so in important transactions requiring full commitment of yourself to the other party, you used your right hand. In Jesus' day, to proffer your right hand meant you were giving your entire self, whether it was to serve or to suffer with someone.[4] Moreover, if you encountered someone of high rank and he put you on his right side, he would be demonstrating that he saw you as worthy of being treated with full dignity.

So why does Jesus say, "If anyone strikes you on your right cheek"? A blow to the right cheek communicated a very specific, negative message. What would this scene look like? You are a slave standing in front of your master, and he is about to strike you. Which hand will he choose?

He can't hit you with his left hand, say the Linns, because it's used only for unclean purposes. So, forced to use his right hand, in order to strike you on the right cheek your master would have to strike you with the *back* of his hand. In that day, hitting someone with the back of your hand was a gesture used by those higher in the pecking order to humiliate those lower. "Masters would backhand slaves, Romans would backhand Jews, husbands would backhand wives and parents would backhand children. The message was, 'Remember your place ... beneath me!'"[5]

If you did what Jesus suggested and turned your left cheek to your tormentor, he would be faced with a dilemma. He can no longer backhand you! Now, in order to use his right hand, he must hit you with his full fist, "a gesture used only between equals.... By turning your other cheek, you have reclaimed your dignity and communicated that you refuse to be humiliated."[6] In addition to making a silent statement that you see yourself as your oppressor's equal, you are also quietly offering him good bread by inviting him to rethink the lie which forms the basis of his arrogance, namely that one man is more valuable than another man.

Hello!

What kind of annual interest rate do your credit cards earn? While some cards offer an initial low rate to get you hooked, rates over 20% are not uncommon on established accounts, especially accounts with retail stores. Financial difficulties often plague those whose sexuality is out of control. In John and Beth's case, they were many thousands of dollars in credit card debt by the time John was ready to deal with his addiction. He has been making the minimum payment on those balances for six years now, and he's paid in much more than the total owed. Yet he's barely made a dent in the balance because of the very high interest rate on those cards. The minimum payment is set up so that it can take decades to actually pay off the original balance. In the meantime, the credit card company is making money hand over fist.

High interest rates were condemned by God in the Old Testament. Usury is a way to permanently transfer wealth from the lower class to the upper class. God despises that kind of exploitation. Jesus addresses this kind of greed in the next part of the passage: "And if anyone wants to sue you and take your undershirt, let him have your coat also."

At that time, rich property owners charged high interest rates on their loans to the poor, knowing all along that the poor would be unable to make the payments. The hope was that the poor would default on the loan. Then the property they had used for collateral would become part of the rich mortgage-holder's estate. Many of the poor had already lost all their property that way. Because of this, if they needed money, they were reduced to offering their clothes as collateral.

Imagine your creditor has brought you to court because you are unable to make your loan payment. The court says, "You owe bigtime. Now hand it over."

The passage in Matthew says he was to give up his "chiton."[7] The "chiton" was a tunic that functioned as an undergarment. Nothing was worn beneath it.

So you are standing before the judge and you have to hand over your underwear. You peel it off and hand it to your creditor. You still have your cloak, so you're not totally naked. Now, Jesus says, go ahead and hand over your cloak, too.

Hello!

Here's the delicious twist to this plot. Back in Jesus' day, it wasn't as scandalous to be seen naked as it was to see someone else naked. By standing before your creditor in the altogether, you are forcing him to experience the humiliation he has caused you.

Walter Wink says, "The creditor is revealed to be not a legitimate moneylender but a party to the reduction of an entire social class to landlessness, destitution, and abasement. This unmasking is not simply punitive, it offers the creditor a chance to see, perhaps for the first time in his life, what his practices cause, and to repent."[8]

Once more, Jesus offers the crowd a way of reclaiming self-respect while at the same time gently offering the oppressor a reality check (good bread) regarding an oppressive economic system.

Make Them Sweat

This last one is kind of fun: "And if any one forces you to go one mile, go with him two miles."

Jesus was talking to a captive people who were compelled to carry very heavy packs for the Roman soldiers. You could be walking along on your way home for supper, and if a Roman soldier came along and wanted a pack mule—tag, you're It. This didn't go over too well. To avoid regular riots, the Romans added a law that said a soldier couldn't force someone to carry a pack for more than one mile. "If the soldier demanded more, he himself could be punished."[9]

So here you are minding your own business and a Roman soldier says, "Hey, you, strap this on your back and walk along behind my horse." You hoist the burden and stumble along until the next mile marker. The soldier is expecting you to drop the load now, but you just keep on walking and whistling.

At first, the soldier thinks maybe you didn't see the mile marker, but you keep going. Now he's starting to get antsy. When are you going to drop the load? You just keep going. His arrogance starts to crumble. *Hey, if anyone sees that he's carrying my pack more than a mile, I could get into big trouble.*

"Look," he says, "you can put it down now."

"No trouble," you reply, marching right along.

Sweat starts dripping down his tunic. *Are there any eyewitnesses who could turn me in?*

"Really, you've carried it far enough," he says, wiping his brow.

"I'm happy to take it a little further for you," you reply, whistling away.

"Please, give it back!" he says, thoroughly flustered and a bit frightened.

For a third time, Jesus offers the people a way to regain their self-respect. A victim would have carried the pack a single mile and gone home bitter that he was forced into servitude. In Jesus' creative solution, generosity overcomes the arrogance of the soldier and you go home chuckling. Meanwhile, you have once more offered your oppressor good bread by quietly confronting the lie that the powerful have the right to requisition the bodies of those under their care.

In each of these stories, someone was victimized by someone else more powerful. Jesus reminded His listeners that even though they might feel powerless in the face of oppressive economic systems, unjust political systems, and tyrannical social systems, they had the greatest power available to anyone—the power to choose their response.

A life of forgiveness is a life of making choices. If there is no choice, we are not exercising forgiveness. Jesus didn't "have" to forgive us. He chose to forgive us. We don't "have" to forgive those who hurt us. We GET to forgive them. We can choose to forgive not because we have to in order to be "good people" but because we want to love. The choice to love God, ourselves, and others empowers us to choose a life of forgiveness.

The Presence of the Table in the Presence of My Enemies

In Psalm 23, David says, "You prepare a table before me in the presence of my enemies. You anoint my head with oil; my cup runs over" (AMPLIFIED).

For a long time, I concentrated on the beginning part of that verse. I thought about how wonderful it was that God was going to give me comfort food right in my enemy's face. I was thrilled to think He would announce His approval of me by anointing my head with oil right while my enemies were watching. Then, one day, I got to wondering about why my cup would run over. Just when you think you understand God, He pulls a fast one on you.

I got to thinking about how at the Last Supper Jesus took the cup, "and when He had given thanks He gave it to them saying, Drink of it, all of you; For this is My blood of the new covenant, which ratifies the agreement and is being poured out for many for the forgiveness of sins."[10] That's when I knew I'd been had.

God sets a table for us in the presence of our enemies not just to feed us but also that we might feed our enemies. He pours the cup of His love for us so full that it spills over and runs down the side of the laden table, across the ground over to where our enemy is standing, and pools at his feet, arresting him with the possibility of abundance. The bouquet of the wine makes his stomach rumble. You motion to him. "Pull up a chair and eat with me. There's more than enough here for the two of us."

To make the point again, in Matthew 18:15-17 Jesus tells His disciples how to handle someone who has wronged us. First, He says, go to him alone and tell him that he's bugged you. If that doesn't work, go back with one or two others so there are eyewitnesses who can vouch for what you said and for how he received you. Finally, just in case he still doesn't listen, take him before the church. If that doesn't work, Jesus says, "Let him be to you as a pagan and a tax collector."

At first glance, it looks like Jesus is saying there are times when it's OK to write someone off. Then you begin remembering how He treated tax collectors and especially wicked sinners. Uh oh! Jesus used to party with that crowd.[11]

This is radical forgiveness and it's not for wimps. You've got to be strong and very courageous to occupy your place with grace, confronting the lie your enemy believes with wit and wisdom. There's only one way you can do this— *you have to know who you are, you have to know that God totally approves of you, you have to be set free from the shame that your enemy is trying to load on you.*

Otherwise, there's a danger that forgiving will degenerate into placating. We're not talking about placating. We're talking about confronting arrogance with generosity.

Where the Rubber Meets the Road

I remember the first time I road-tested radical forgiveness. Someone had viciously gossiped about me. She caused me harm intentionally, and there were some serious repercussions from the gossip. I decided to be holy and pray for her.

Then one day I heard she and her family were sick with the flu. The next morning when I was praying for her, the Lord told me to fix her a meal. "No way," I said. "Praying for her is all I can manage." Then the Lord reminded me to "bless those who curse you and do good to those who hate you."

"Forget it," I said.

"Be not overcome with evil, but overcome evil with good," He said.

"All right!"

So I fixed a lovely meal and groused in the car all the way over to her house. When I got there, I said, "God, if You don't show up and give me the grace to go up that driveway, there's no way I can get out of this car." So He showed up. Typical.

I walked up the steps and rang the bell. When she opened the door, I suddenly understood.

The look on her face when she saw me standing there with a beautiful meal made it all quite worthwhile. "If your enemy be hungry, give him bread to eat, and if he be thirsty, give him water to drink; for so doing you will heap coals of fire on his head and the Lord will reward you."[12] No, we never became friends, but I went away whole and she was left to struggle with her conscience.

It's not always wise to do good to an enemy in person. In another situation, a woman was greatly betrayed by a friend. Because of the nature of the offense, she wisely cut off the relationship. For a long time she was hurt and then she was angry and then she was very angry and then she got worried about herself because she couldn't seem to stop being angry. One day, she remembered Proverbs 21:14: "A gift in secret pacifieth anger." So when she felt angry, she secretly gave a gift to this former friend. She discovered that her anger melted before her generosity. After that, whenever she felt the anger coming back, she would give a secret gift. In time, not only did her anger subside but she was able to smile when she saw this person.

In another situation, a woman found a creative way to give good bread to her husband, who was a recovering sex addict. He was no longer acting out, so sexual relations would have been safe, but she felt angry because the only time he talked to her or looked at her was during sex. He didn't seem to be able to have a relationship with her apart from sex. She felt as if she was being objectified. She talked to a friend. "I don't get it. Why is this the only time he wants to be with me? I feel so rejected," she said.

"Don't look at it that way," the friend counseled. "Look at it as the only way into his soul."

After thinking it over, the woman decided she would aggressively pursue her husband's soul through his body. When, during their lovemaking, he would say or do something that echoed of the pornography he had been involved with, she would gently but firmly say, "That's not OK, but this is," and then she would make love to him in healthy ways.

Slowly, her husband began to open his soul to her at other times. He began to look her in the eye, and he began to talk with her outside the bedroom. It took a lot of courage, but she kept inviting him to the banqueting table and reminding herself that the banner over him was love.

Another woman struggled desperately because of her husband's lying. He had gotten into the lying habit during his years as an addict and now, even though he was recovering, the character deficiency remained. He would lie about anything; it didn't have to be something important. Most troubling for her was when he would lie in front of others. She didn't want to dishonor her husband, but she knew that her silence was complicity, which dishonored him too. She was also worried about how she would be perceived if she corrected her husband in public. So, after much prayer, she decided that she would have to die to what other people thought of her and creatively offer her husband good bread.

"I can't enable your lying any longer," she told him one day. "The next time you lie to someone in my presence, I'm going to interrupt the conversation and tell him that you've made a lot of progress in your recovery, but that you still have a difficult time telling the truth. Then I'm going to tell him that I've made a commitment to walk through this with you by speaking up whenever you fall back into your old ways." The next time they were out in public, her husband began to tell a lie, looked over at his wife, and caught her eye. She smiled. He quickly changed his story and told the truth.

For the Joy Set Before Us

So, how do you find the courage to offer this good bread? The same way Jesus did. "He, for the joy set before Him, endured the cross, despising the shame."[13] What was the "joy set before Him"? At the Transfiguration, the Father told Peter, James, and John what it was: "This is my beloved

Son, in whom I am well pleased."[14]

Jesus had His Father's love and approval, and that's all He needed to leap over tall piles of shame with a single bound, offering good bread to the very ones who had tried to heap the shame upon Him. The joy He feels from experiencing His Father's approval snatches the shame out of His enemies' taunts and so empowers Him that He invites His shamers to the banqueting table.

There was only one moment in His life on earth when Jesus didn't feel the love and approval of His Father. It was that killing moment on the cross when God had to turn His back on His Son because His Son had just become sin and a Holy God cannot approve of sin. In that moment of abandonment, Jesus cried, "My God. My God. Why have you forsaken me?" And, then He died. In a very real sense, many of our children die inside when their fathers withhold their love and approval.

This sense of being deeply loved and approved of in the presence of your enemies, is the oil that anoints the mourner in Psalm twenty-three. Oil is the symbol of the Holy Spirit. When the Spirit comes, He comes speaking of the Father's love and approval. When Jesus was baptized and the heavens opened and the Holy Spirit descended like a dove, what did the Father say? "This is my beloved Son, in Whom I am well pleased."[15] The anointing breaks the yoke of shame, not because the yoke is suddenly made weaker, but because you suddenly become much bigger and stronger. You awake out of your slumber of shame with shouts of joy. Now you can pour a cup of wine and let it spill over the table and down the sides and pool at your enemy's feet. You can set out fresh bread and motion him over. "Pull up a chair. There's plenty at this table."

Thinking It Through

1. How have faulty understandings of the Matthew 5 passage kept you thinking in the victim mode? What has been the result?

2. Can you think of a time when someone offered you good bread by performing an act of generosity that challenged your arrogance? What happened inside you?

3. Which relationship provides your greatest challenge? How can you have fun confronting the disease in that relationship?

4. Do you know that you have your heavenly Father's love and full approval? If not, what seems to block you from receiving it?

PART THREE

Dealing With
the Ongoing Realities

FIFTEEN

The Gates Are Down, the Lights Are Flashing, but the Train is Nowhere in Sight

Praying is no easy matter. It demands a relationship in which you allow the other to enter into the very center of your person, allow him to speak there, allow im to touch the sensitive core of your being and allow him to see so much that you would rather leave in darkness. And when do you want to do that? Perhaps you would let the other come across the threshold to say something, to touch something, but to let him into that place where your life gets its form, that is dangerous and calls for defense.[1]

Henri Nouwen

Look at me. I stand at the door. I knock. If you hear me call and open the door, I'll come right in and sit down to supper with you.

REVELATION 3:20, THE MESSAGE

Go back with me for a moment, to that synagogue in Nazareth, before the crowd got all bent out of shape because Jesus wasn't going to perform for them. He is standing up as the Isaiah scroll is handed to Him. Let the words He reads sink into your soul:

The Spirit of the Lord is upon Me, because He has anointed me to preach the good news to the poor; He has sent Me to announce release to the captives and recovery of sight to the blind, to send forth as delivered those who are oppressed—who are downtrodden, bruised, crushed, and broken down by calamity, To proclaim the accepted and acceptable year of the Lord—the day when salvation and the free favors of God profusely abound.[2]

With this reading, Jesus announced that the gospel went far beyond mere intellectual understanding. To Him, the Kingdom wasn't just something you experienced from your neck up. With Jesus, the Kingdom of God was something you could touch and taste and smell and see. So, while Isaiah probably never suspected that he wrote the mission statement for Jesus' ministry, even Stephen Covey couldn't have crafted a better one.

The Kingdom of God Is Among You

Jesus' mission statement wasn't mere words. Jesus delivered. And because He delivered, He attracted the most broken members of society. If what He had had to say was mere head-knowledge without any profound impact on their innermost being, these people wouldn't have given Him the time of day.

In the Western world, we make the gospel an intellectual activity. Because we don't see the radical transformations Scripture says happened when Jesus touched lives, we tell ourselves it is enough to inform the mind of who God is and how He works, hoping against hope that the accumulation of facts will somehow make us holy. We learn the tribal customs of the church and tie on works of righteousness. But underneath it all, our souls are screaming for living water. We wonder how long we'll have to pretend that this desert we're crawling through is a Club Med vacation.

Meanwhile, we miss the main point: Christianity is not a garment. It's a habitation. When the Kingdom of God really comes to us, a personal transformation occurs that is evident to us and to those who know us. When the blind can see and the poor get rich and the captives are freed and the brokenhearted are healed, they *know* they've been touched by the Living God. They *know* they've entered into the Kingdom, and so does everyone around them.

Laughing on the Outside and Crying on the Inside

The intellectual gospel works when you're not too badly broken. It works for those who are healthy enough to adopt the habit of Christianity. They learn the secret handshake. They get rid of their bad habits. They develop good habits. This is a form of godliness without the power thereof, but it does work. Habit Christianity gives us a society that has some measure of salt in it because we're behaving well with each other.

The addict and the codependent try the gospel according to the self-help movement. They learn how to admit that they're powerless to save themselves, and they turn over their lives to God. They learn how to take responsibility for their actions and how to make restitution to those they've harmed. This is coping-mechanism Christianity, and it can help to stabilize lives that are out of control, and that is very good.

But Christianity is not a habit. It is not a coping mechanism. Christianity is about being broken into. It is about being invaded to the core of our being by a God who fully knows and fully loves us. Neither of which we really believe—but both of which our hearts desperately hope could be true. In the gospel, we return to Eden, that place of being fully known and fully loved. Only this is not an Eden on the outside, this is an Eden on the inside, planted in the garden of our hearts.

Sin locked us out of the Garden. Forgiveness is the key that swings open the gate so we can once more eat of the Tree of Life. So, the linchpin of the gospel is forgiveness.

Forgiveness is about getting a heart transplant. "A new heart will I give you and a new spirit will I put within you, and I will take away the stony heart out of your flesh and give you a heart of flesh. And I will put my Spirit within you and cause you to walk in My statutes, and you shall heed My ordinances, and do them. And you shall dwell in the land that I gave to your fathers; and you shall be My people, and I will be your God. I will also save you from all your uncleannesses."[3]

This is the Ark of the Covenant put inside us. In the Old Covenant, the Law was carved into the flesh of a stone. In the New Covenant, the law carves stone into flesh. The law comes like a plough bit. It cuts deep into our hearts, showing us where we need to forgive and be forgiven.

Because the law is so useful in cultivating our hearts, some mistake it for that which gives our hearts life. The law is not the water our thirsty hearts long for. It is only an implement whose piercing action releases the spring of life hidden in the stony places where we have hardened ourselves off.

The law does this by giving us the knowledge of good (that which follows the law) and evil (that which breaks the law). Trying to obtain this knowledge apart from their relationship with God is what got Adam and Eve kicked out of the Garden. By writing His laws in our hearts, God shows us He has forgiven us our presumption and once again establishes Himself as the Bread which can feed every longing of our hearts.

By writing His laws in our hearts, God once again gives us dominion in the earth, because now that we know how to rightly divide the word of truth, we are equipped to rule and reign with Him. By writing His laws in our hearts, God re-creates our hearts in His own image and likeness—thus redeeming Satan's lie that knowing good and evil will make us like gods. Now the living water starts to bubble up within us and we are able to refresh those who are thirsting. This is why the psalmist says, "The law of the Lord is perfect, restoring the whole person."[4]

That Ol' Achy Breaky Heart

So this begs the question, what is the heart? In the Old Covenant, the word for heart, *lev*, means our deepest, innermost feelings. In the New Covenant, the word for heart, *kardia*, means the seat and center of human life. The heart is where we live. It's the wellspring out of which our life flows. Here our conscience speaks. Here our gut sense of intuition dwells. Here is the seat of our will. Here we are capable of intimacy with God and others. "And there I will meet with thee, and I will commune with thee."[5]

We can break our own hearts by refusing to make the proper decision. Scripture calls this "hardening our hearts." We shut off the alarm of our conscience, disregard our intuition, close our eyes to the breech this choice will make in our personal relationships, and plunge headlong over the cliff of selfishness in our desperate pursuit of bread. Such wanton disregard for the health of our heart is risky business and always leaves a trail of rock-hard scar tissue.

Some of us have had our hearts broken by those who lust after our bread.

Knowing that if they asked we wouldn't give them what they want, the lusters bypass our security systems, climb in the one window that wasn't locked, and cart off as much bread as their greedy little pockets can hold. Fearful of being broken into again, we board up the windows of our soul and nail shut the doors into our heart, thus hardening ourselves to both the pain and the possibilities.

The psalmists spoke often about the devastating results of wounds to the heart:

> For the enemy has persecuted my soul; he has crushed my life to the ground; he has made me dwell in dark places, like those who have long been dead. Therefore, my spirit is overwhelmed within me; my heart is appalled within me.
>
> PSALM 143:3,4, AMPLIFIED

> Reproach has broken my heart, and I am so sick. And I looked for comforters and there were none.
>
> PSALM 69:20, AMPLIFIED

> For I am afflicted and needy, and my heart is wounded within me.
>
> PSALM 109:22, AMPLIFIED

If we comb through Scripture and distill the passages that talk about brokenheartedness down to their essence, we learn that brokenheartedness is characterized by three things: broken faith, crushed hopes, and ambivalence about love.

Broken Faith

The Ants in the Pants That Keep Faith Moving

How do you define faith? Do you think people who have faith have an inside track on God? Do you suspect they've been given the secret message decoder so that there are no mysteries about how life is unfolding before them? Dan Allender says that most people define faith as an absence of doubt, a lack of confusion. We think that if we have faith we'll know what to do. But, the truth is, unless you involve people in doubt, they will never grow in faith.[6] Doubts, Frederick Beuchner says, are "the ants in the pants that keep faith moving."[7]

Faith expresses itself in doubt when something in our world is amiss. Something is different from the way we're sure God wants it to be. The recognition that things are not right comes from our understanding of who God is and how He works. The psalmist cries out, "God, I know you're like this but my life is like that. I don't get it. How come you're not acting like yourself?"

Abraham and Sarah certainly struggled this way. They knew God had promised them a child. Yet, month after month, there was no conception. When the months turned into years and the years into decades, they began to doubt. "Abraham, I know God is able to give us a child," Sarah said one day as she fixed her husband a Reuben sandwich. "Doesn't He like us anymore or did we miss something in the translation?"

Faith Will Not Grow Without an Entrance Into the Past[8]

Our faith in God and our faith in man are intertwined. If others have let us down, it is next to impossible not to harbor a secret fear that God will, too. For this reason, faith will not grow without an entrance into the past because the past is where our trust has been broken. We must follow the crumbs of our doubts back in time until we come to the place where our bread fell out of our basket.

Our past is made up of memories, short stories actually, the facts of which are often quite blurry. When it comes to the way we interpret our lives, the facts of our stories don't move us. What moves us is what the stories told us about our place in this world.

A while back, a woman revisited the stories of all the times her husband arrived home with their one car too late for her and her children to make their appointments.

"I found myself over the years drifting into a pattern of frustration, covered by niceness, outbursts, and then finally defeat. Because of his repeated lateness, I began to not prepare to leave on time, so that when the car finally arrived, I wasn't ready to go. Of course, I was chastised for not being ready and making myself even later than was necessary (so it wasn't all his fault). But anyone getting babies ready to go knows that changing the outfit too far ahead is a waste, and besides the fifteen minutes he said he would be late sometimes stretched into an hour.

"I found myself having anxiety at every need to go out, every appointment or social invitation. Would I make it on time or be embarrassed? I began to show up late for things or not go. Eventually I became more and more isolated. The effort was just too hard. I didn't care if I was late anymore, and like my husband, I blamed my disrespect for other people's time as their problem with being nit-picky. I could see myself sliding, but the countersolution, to be unsubmissive and disrespectful to my husband, seemed too big a trade-off."

This woman's accumulated stories had stopped her in her tracks. The shame she felt about her powerlessness in the face of someone else's irresponsibility killed her faith in the future.

Entering Into the Groanings of Our Heart

Moving into the stories of our lives is not about nostalgia. Nostalgia gives us the warm fuzzies, but airbrushing reality will not help us deal with our doubts.[9] As we go back and reread our stories, the hard questions that we have been running from jump off the pages and confront us with doubt.

The young woman who, starry-eyed, married her sweetheart only to discover a few months into the marriage that her husband has a secret addiction to pornography, may have also years earlier discovered her dad's own private stash and vowed that she would never, ever marry a man who would be like her dad. And now, here she is and what does that tell her about whether "happily ever after" will ever be true for her?

Parents find drugs in the room of the child they tried so hard to do everything right for. And what does that tell them about whether or not they know how to love their child?

A young man has a knock-down-drag-out with his dad. This is only the latest skirmish in their ongoing battle to feel loved and respected by the other. Neither can risk saying, "I love you. What can we do to make things work between us?" for fear the other will say, "Don't bother. Now that I've seen the worst of you, I don't think I can love you." Meanwhile, each retires to his own corner and wonders whether these repeated battles really mean they will never find the love and acceptance their hearts cry for.

What about you? Did God give you a promise He seems to be slow in keeping? Have people repeatedly broken their word to you? What doubts has your story given you?

The more we doubt, the less we trust. And, of course, this is the way evil works. Evil knows that without faith it is impossible to please God—not because it's not possible to please Him but because the faithless man cannot feel the pleasure God has in him. He has learned too many times that people don't mean what they say and there's no sense risking something as important as heaven by having blind faith in the mere declaration of peace on earth, good will toward men with whom He is well pleased. It might not be true. So the faithless man can never quite cease striving.

Yet, God welcomes our doubts because doubts are honest questions and He is an honest God. He invites us to doubt our presuppositions because sometimes we're going at things the wrong way and we need to learn that we've been using the wrong secret decoder ring. Doubt also gives us an opportunity to re-examine our assumptions about who God is, because sometimes we're worshiping a household idol, not the true and living God.

As the events of our lives are remembered and our doubts are expressed, we enter into the emotions of our stories. This is why, in addition to containing stories of past events, the Psalms are so full of emotions. "I remember God; I am disquieted and I groan; I muse in prayer, and my spirit faints— overwhelmed."[10] The psalmist reminds us that to revisit our stories is to enter into the groanings of our heart. This wisdom is repeated in the New Testament. Romans 8, the chapter that is so often quoted as the answer for the believer's doubts, is full of groanings—the groanings of creation, the groanings of travail, the groanings that are too deep for uttering. "Getting in touch with your emotions" is not a recent invention of therapists and counselors.[11]

Crushed Hopes

Art worked for the same company for almost thirty years. His integrity and graciousness toward others won him the deep respect of his peers. In time, he rose to the rank of vice president and traveled all over the world making excellent deals for his company. His business acumen was widely recognized and he was mentioned a number of times in well-respected publications as a man with a profound grasp of his industry. His achievements meant that he generated a very healthy income, a portion of which he saved and invested wisely.

His family had a very happy life. They had a vacation home in Maine which gave them many happy memories. They laughed regularly with good friends. They gave generously to their community and to the less fortunate. Then, one day, the company changed hands, and someone walked into Art's office and told him his type of leadership was no longer wanted. Instead, they wanted someone more cutthroat. Someone who might be willing to stack the deck a bit if it meant a sweeter deal. Someone who looked at the short-term bottom line rather than the long-term health of the company or the best interests of the client.

For a moment Art tottered, and then he regained his balance and decided to use some of his expertise to go into consulting. But then the bottom dropped out of the market and his prospects vanished. He lost his confidence that he knew how to do anything well and right because doing things well and right had put him in this crazy place. He wondered what the new definition of well and right was, and he felt he would be betraying all he believed about life if he started playing the game the way the corporate headhunters told him it was played today.

To save money, he and his wife sold their home and moved to their beloved Maine retreat full-time. Eventually, after working and reworking their finances, they had to sell their dream because they could no longer afford the taxes. The couple who bought it gutted it and built a bigger place. Watching the place they loved be dismantled, Art and his wife wondered how their lives could have turned out like this. Now Art struggles with depression, and his personality changes have put a severe strain on his marriage.

When life throws us curveball after curveball, we stop living in the moment because the moment, with all its disappointed hopes, seems too painful to grasp. We are always just hoping for tomorrow, tomorrow. After all, it's only a day away. Believing that if we just make the right choices, tomorrow will bring the hope we so long for, we keep slogging through difficult todays.

When, despite our best efforts, we accumulate a number of todays that are no different than yesterday, we begin to wonder if maybe God has turned His back on us. Surely, if He found us worthy, He would bless our efforts and life would get on track. Surely, if He loved us, He would put an end to our misery. When the heavens are brass, hope dies that tomorrow will ever be any different than today. We now dive headlong into the abyss of despair.

Faith grows through grappling with doubt, and hope grows through an entry into despair. We face despair as the addict we love recycles into his addiction. We face despair as the marriage we worked so hard to save ends up in the divorce court. We face despair when the in-law we work so hard to love continues to turn his or her back on us.

We grow up believing that if we give our best to the world, the best will come back to us. Despair comes when we learn that our best has actually snatched hope from us. And, of course, this is what evil hopes for. Because just as the faithless man has lost his ability to believe in the goodness of God, the hopeless man has lost his ability to believe that the goodness of God has come to make His habitation in him. And once a man is robbed of that hope, he has no way to disarm evil because evil is only disarmed through goodness.

Ambivalent Love

The Bottom Line

Faith and hope are intimately related. Faith is about how things have or have not worked out for us in the past. Hope is about how things will or will not work out for us in the future. The one who controls the past controls the future, and the one who controls the future owns the present because we make our present-day decisions based on our perceptions of what the future holds.[12]

This is why it's so important that Jesus Christ is the same yesterday, today, and forever. He is simultaneously in our past, our present, and our future. He is where we were, where we are, and where we will be. He is the only One who can say that to us.

With Him in charge, we are able to risk going back into our past because we are safe with Him and we know He has already made good plans for us, plans for a future and a hope. ("For I know the plans I have for you, says the Lord, plans for good and not for evil, to give you a future and a hope."[13])

So, if the past is about faith and the future is about hope, what is the present about? Love. Love is about how we handle today. And here we come up against the ultimate purpose of evil. Evil breaks our faith and crushes our hopes because once trust and hope are destroyed, we become fearful about love. ("And because iniquity shall abound, the love of many shall wax cold."[14])

The husband who delights to give good gifts to his wife finds his ardor quenched when nothing he does pleases her. The woman who lights a lamp in the window to welcome her husband home, finds the light in her heart snuffed out when she discovers that while she was lighting the lamp, her husband was with another woman.

Our bruising experiences with hope and trust have taught us that it is not safe to love. Evil knows that as long as it hurts to love, we will always be ambivalent about our affections for others. We will never quite dig in and woo their hearts with goodness. We will never quite trust others to woo ours. Our hearts become tentative instead of tenacious.

We lose the courage to enter the arena.

Herein lies one of the myths of love. We have thought that the more we loved, the more peaceful our outer life would be, but Matthew 10 makes it clear that the more we love, the more we are willing to engage in the battle for the hearts and souls of men.

Not long ago, I spoke with a woman who didn't know what it meant to love her husband in the midst of his recovery from an addiction. She loved him dearly, but she was fearful of being hurt because she had no assurance that he would continue to get better. When things were going well, she was afraid to let herself hope because she was always waiting for the other shoe to drop. Because she wasn't sure if it was wise to give room for hope, she withheld her affections in the present. Yet, she saw his many fine qualities and longed to love him. She realized her ambivalence was destroying the possibility the marriage could be healed, but she was powerless to silence her fears.

When our hearts are tentative, we become ambivalent about love. Ambivalence is a nasty state of being. In order to survive it, we have to break off the part of our heart that is too painful to face. In that compartmentalization, we become the double-minded man that James talks about.[15] Unstable in all our ways, we are fearful of approaching love, yet at the same time we are reluctant to avoid it. There is no way God can answer our prayers because we are asking for two opposite things. Kill him, God. Make him whole, God.

The gates are down, the lights are flashing, but the train is nowhere in sight.

"Thou shalt love the Lord thy God with all thy heart, soul, mind and strength and thy neighbor as thyself."[16] God's kingdom comes to earth as we love one another. Why would evil seek to destroy love? Because where love is, God is.[17] If evil can make us ambivalent about love by destroying our ability to trust and hope, it might be able to obliterate the presence of God on the face of the earth.

"And now abideth faith, hope and love, these three: but the greatest of these is love."[18]

THE READER: "I have a question before we end this thing. Are you saying that love requires us to stay in bad situations? You've been talking about forgiving with bread, and now you're talking about being tenacious in love. Does God expect us to hang in there no matter what the betrayal or injustice?"

LAURIE: "Thanks for giving me a chance to clarify things. In this chapter I haven't been talking so much about the requirements of love as I have the consequences of sin. We can choose our actions, but we can't choose our consequences. Sin sets in motion a chain of consequences that break trust, crush hopes, and quench love. Knowing that, we are to do what we can to guard our heart from influences that destroy it."

THE READER: "So what you're really saying is repeated betrayals and injustices break the marriage covenant into a million pieces. And our family gets their hearts broken in the fallout."

LAURIE: "Right. Covenant gives us the authority to extract strong consequences for such behavior in the hopes that our spouse will see the light and be restored to God, to himself or herself, and to us. Love requires that we exercise that authority. But giving good bread isn't about setting yourself up for further abuse. Proverbs 22:3 tells us, 'A prudent man sees the evil and hides himself, but the simple pass on and are punished with suffering'" (AMPLIFIED).

THE READER: "How long should you wait to see if the relationship can be healed?"

LAURIE: The heart knows how long it can wait. Those who wait a long time are not holier than those who don't. And those who leave sooner rather than later are not necessarily healthier than those who stay. Choosing to stay for today doesn't mean you are required to stay for tomorrow. These things are best done one day at a time."

THE READER: "Can you foresee any time when it would be wise to leave?"

LAURIE: "I think it's wise to leave when you know staying is keeping the spouse from dealing with his or her issues or when you or your children are in physical danger. I think it's imperative to leave if your children have been sexually abused by your spouse. Mercy requires that we protect the vulnerable. So it's a parent's job to protect the children, even if that means protecting them from their other parent."

THE READER: "That sounds kind of unforgiving."

LAURIE: "Forgiving someone does not relieve them of having to face the consequences of their actions."

THE READER: "Are you saying that even if you were willing to forgive over and over and love unconditionally year in and year out, not every relationship can be healed?"

LAURIE: "Forgiveness is unconditional love that flows from a heart set free of shame. That love flows no matter what the other person does about it. But reconciliation depends on the other party being willing to change the destructive behavior. You can choose to forgive even if the other person doesn't repent; but reconciliation takes two. Forgiveness is the way you set yourself free from the pain of the past; repentance is the way your offender sets you free to hope for the future of the relationship. Forgiveness allows you to keep the vows you made to love, honor, and cherish someone even if prudence dictates that you no longer do it in the married state."

Thinking It Through

1. What do your stories tell you about your place in this world?

2. What is the hardest thing for you to trust? Where did your bread fall out of your basket?

3. Scripture says when we are living as sinners we are like dead men walking (Eph 2:1). Dead men don't think and they don't feel. They're totally disengaged from *real* life. Scripture also says that emotional numbness precedes sexual brokenness (Eph 4:17-20).

How has your own sin or the sin of others numbed your heart? How has that numbness affected your sexual choices? Think of a time when you wanted to do something you knew was wrong. What kind of mind games did you play with yourself so you wouldn't have to think about what you were getting ready to do? How about later? How did you shut off your mind and silence your emotions so you wouldn't have to think or feel emotions about what you had done? Did it work? Did you find that the more you refused to think and feel the easier it was to sin? What finally woke you up?

4. What parts of yourself have you broken off because they were just too painful to look at? How has the resulting ambivalence affected your ability to love?

SIXTEEN

Growing Flowers on
the Manure Piles of Life

Up to a point, a man's life is shaped by environment,
heredity and movements and changes in the world about
him; then, there comes a time when it lies within his grasp
to shape the clay of his life into the sort of thing he wants
to be. Only the weak blame parents, their race, their
times, lack of good fortune, or the quirks of fate. Everone
has it within his power to say, this I am today, that I shall
be tomorrow. The wish, however, must be implemented by
deeds.

Louis L'Amour

They overcame the accuser of the brethren by the blood of
the lamb and by the word of their testimony; and the loved
not their lives unto death.

REVELATION 12:11

Earlier today, I took a walk down our country road. It was an absolutely
glorious afternoon, just enough nip in the air for a nice thick sweatshirt,
but just enough warm sun to keep me from having to don a jacket. Jacket days
are coming, though: the hills across from our barn are splashed with reds and
oranges, and that means chicken soup and flannel sheets can't be too far
behind.

Actually, they may be sooner than I thought when I wrote that first
paragraph: Steve just came in and told me it's 38 degrees outside. He whis-

pered rumors of snow. I said, "No way. It's only the first of October." He just laughed. He was right: outside my office window, the fluffy stuff has started to fall.

Guess I'll have to admit it, summer is past, harvest is over, and winter is coming. That's OK, we're ready for her. Out back, our wood is stacked, ready for the continual fires we'll soon be keeping in our two woodstoves. I always look forward to the smell of the smoke and the warmth of the hearth.

Down cellar, in the big freezer, the chickens I wrote about in chapter ten are ready for roasting or making into pies or soup. I've decided it's been way too many years since chicken, celery, and onions simmered all night on our big woodstove. So, when I finish this chapter, I'm getting out our big stock pots and laying in a winter's worth of chicken stock. By the way, don't feel bad for the chickens. They had a happy life before it was time for that 4:30 A.M. chicken roundup.

Chicken manure is about the best stuff going when it comes to fertilizing your garden. So, out back behind the barn, the chickens' final gift to us is quietly composting, waiting for the gardening season that I know will come after this winter is past.

Here's the tricky part about chicken manure: if you use it before it's well-composted, the nitrogen in it will burn your garden instead of feeding it. You have to kind of watch it and make sure everything is well rotted down.

It's kind of like that with the manure piles in our lives. Sometimes, some-one drives into our yard and dumps a bucket load of the stuff all over us, and for a while it's so hot, it burns anything that tries to grow on it. But if we give it time to compost down, we find we've got something so rich we can grow unbelievably beautiful flowers on top of it.

Movin' On Out and Up

We know we are progressing down the road of radical forgiveness when we stop asking for an explanation for the chaos of our lives and start planning what we are going to make with it. Don't get me wrong, there's nothing wrong with asking, "What made this mess?" We need to do that in order to figure out exactly what has happened to us. But as long as we stay in the diag-nostic mode, all we are doing is walking around the manure pile.

"Yep, that sure is a pile and it sure does stink," we say to ourselves. So far, so good. Now, let it compost, because we are created in the image of a God who never wastes the waste. Instead, out of the meaninglessness, He creates beautiful, wonderful things. He invites us to do the same. But getting there is a process, and it often takes a winter or two.

When someone sins against you, he or she takes you by forced march from the place where you want to be to a place you never even thought of going. That is the nature of sin. It seeks to usurp our place, destroy our person, and kill our passion.

In the early stages of forgiveness, we spend a lot of time in the middle of the pile desperately shoveling, hoping to get back to square one so we can recover our place, regain our rights, and reclaim our passion.

After exhausting ourselves and getting pretty stinky to boot, we begin to realize that part of forgiveness is *accepting* the fact that the sin has changed everything. The child is dead. The job is gone. The marriage is over. The friendship has ended. The trust has been destroyed. The balloon of our illusions has been popped. Now we are ready to fall into the ground and die to our old way of life.

The dying is rarely painless and rarely quick. And that is all right. Dying to the old is like moving from the neighborhood where you grew up. After all, you lived there forever and you've never lived here before. So, you're always talking about "back when we lived in Cincinnati." Reminisce away. But, keep learning about your new neighborhood. Keep trying out those new behaviors. Keep exploring those new thoughts and feelings and understandings. Keep opening yourself to the gifts of life. In time, you'll find beautiful, wonderful things starting to sprout from the compost.

Candy Lightner made something beautiful and wonderful out of the senseless loss of a child when she founded Mothers Against Drunk Driving. Barbara Johnson founded Spatula Ministries and wrote a number of best-selling books after going through the horrific experience of burying two sons and losing a third to a homosexual lifestyle. John Walsh's six-year-old son Adam was abducted in 1981 and later found murdered. John and his wife Reve have gone on to become tireless advocates for victims' rights and missing children. John is host of the TV show, *America's Most Wanted: America Fights Back,* and the author of several books.

Candy, Barbara, and John are overcomers. They let their pain compost down and then grew beautiful, wonderful things on the manure piles in their lives. They processed through the "My God, My God, why hast thou forsaken me?" victim phase of forgiveness, past the "It is finished" resignation stage of forgiveness, to the "I am ascending to My Father and your Father, and to My God and your God" resurrection phase of forgiveness. In very real ways, they fell into the ground and died to their old way of life so that they could open themselves to the possibility that good could come out of the evil. They accepted the gift of bread. Having eaten, they set the banqueting table for others.

Fully embracing God's sovereignty is the only way I can find the courage to set the banqueting table. Otherwise, everything I do is only a reaction to the chaos, a frantic bullet-dodging exercise. By acknowledging God's sovereignty, I accept that even though things in my world are out of my control, they are fully in God's control. Somehow, in some way, they are part of the story He is writing in my life and therefore they can be embraced as teachers rather than fought against as if they were subjugators.

You CAN Get There From Here

When we stop shoveling the pile and start letting it compost down, we realize we can no longer ignore the depth of our emotional wounds, nor can we limit forgiveness merely to exploring those wounds and putting up boundaries to avoid future violations. We have to learn the riskiness of forgiveness. After all, love comes without guarantee of warm reception or reciprocation. It has an element of powerlessness. We can't control the outcome. To cast your bread upon the waters and not know when it will come back to you is to fall into the abyss of trust—and you have already learned that man cannot be trusted. This is the tension of forgiveness.

Take a page from Jesus' book. He knew human nature, therefore He did not trust Himself to men.[1] Instead, He trusted Himself to God, and that trust gave Him the complete confidence that those who would love Him would love Him: "All whom My Father gives to Me will come to Me."[2] He knew it was not about Him being enough. He was who He is, "I am the Bread of Life." Instead, it is about us knowing we are hungry enough and thirsty enough to be willing to pull up a chair at the banqueting table He spreads before us. "He who comes to Me will never be hungry, and he who believes in and cleaves to and trusts in and relies on Me will never thirst any more at any time."[3]

This is the stunning way back into the Garden. Remember that Adam and Eve wanted to be like God, who knows the thoughts and intents of our hearts. They saw the power of that, so they ate the fruit from the Tree of the Knowledge of Good and Evil. And sure enough, they became like God. They "knew" each other's hearts, and that knowing caused them to feel such shame that they no longer felt right about themselves. So they hid from their God and they hid from each other. In their hiding place, they tried to justify themselves by lobbing accusations at each other.

In forgiveness, the linkage between shame and sin are forever broken by the One who endured the cross for us. He despised the shame so that we might not grow weary in our trials or lose our hearts in the battle.[4]

In forgiveness, the linkage between the Knowledge of Good and Evil and judgment are forever broken. We no longer need to hide from the shame of what others think of us or the shame of what we think of ourselves because the withered fig leaves we have used to cover up our failures have been replaced by a full-length coat woven from the wool of the Lamb. The label inside reads, "Handmade especially for you with love, so drop the pretenses."

In forgiveness, we become "like" God in a new way. We receive the mind of Christ and the Spirit of Truth who will guide us into all truth. Therefore, we become "the spiritual man" who "tries all things, examines, investigates, inquires into, questions, and discerns all things, yet is himself to be put on trial and judged by no one. For who has known or understood the mind, the counsels and purposes, of the Lord so as to guide and instruct Him and give Him knowledge? But we have the mind of Christ and do hold the thoughts and feelings and purposes of His heart."[5]

What are the thoughts and feelings and purposes of God's heart? They are tied up in the fulfillment of a covenantal promise He made at the foundation of the world, while Adam and Eve were standing there trembling over the horror of their discovery of what it means to be "like" God. "I'm going to give this woman you deceived an Offspring who will bruise and tread your head underfoot," God told Satan. "And you will lie in wait and bruise His heel."[6]

"For God so greatly loved and dearly prized the world that He even gave up His only begotten Son, so that whoever believes in, trusts in, clings to, and relies on Him shall not perish but have eternal life. For God did not send the Son into the world in order to judge, reject, condemn, or pass sentence on the world, but that the world might find salvation and be made safe and sound through Him. He who believes in Him is not judged. He who trusts in Him never comes up for judgment; for him, there is no rejection, no condemnation; but he who does not believe is judged already because he has not believed in and trusted in the name of the only begotten Son of God. He is condemned for refusing to let his trust rest in Christ's name" because "there is no other place you can find safety from the scrutiny."[7]

Now we have moved from the powerlessness of love to the power of love. The pile has been composted and from its rich soil, good wheat has been grown and sweet grapes have been plucked. So firmly convinced of who we are that we don't we have to argue about our worth or hold on to our position, we strip off our agendas, take up the towel, and wash the feet of those who are about to disappoint us in big ways.

It's time to throw a few more logs on the fire and make the chicken stock. The banquet is about to begin.

One Last Thing ...

We've been on quite a journey together. I've tried to think of this book as a cup of tea and a chat with you, the reader. So for that reason, around my computer, I've posted pictures and letters sent to me by readers of *An Affair of the Mind*. I have frequently paused in my writing to reread your stories and touch your faces.

I don't feel I can leave you without mentioning one more thing about forgiveness: extreme betrayals cause extreme reactions. God didn't call certain things "sin" because He doesn't want us to have any fun. He labeled certain actions "sin" because of the devastation they wreak in lives. One of those devastations is post-traumatic stress disorder. You might have heard of PTSD in war veterans where it's often called "shell shock." If someone has waged war on your soul through extreme betrayal, you may experience your own version of "shell shock."

That's because memories of traumas are stored in our cells. They are chemically burned into our brains, and they show up as diseases in our bodies. Women who undergo abortion are more likely to develop breast cancer. Women who experience sexual abuse have higher incidences of breast, uterine, and cervical cancer, and if the abuse involved oral sex, cancers of the mouth and throat as well as TMJ. Auto-immune diseases are also more frequent among abuse victims. Even if you aren't a victim of abuse, you may have experienced a profound trauma, and the memories of that trauma may be causing severe personality changes and sicknesses in your body. For this reason, processing traumatic memories is a crucial part of forgiveness.

I Am Shut Up and Cannot Come Forth

My own dark night of the soul began after a terrifying traumatic experience. This experience occurred at a time when I was physically exhausted and emotionally spent. I made some good decisions about how to handle this, and I also made some dumb ones. I removed myself from a bad situation and began working through to forgiveness. But somehow, my body didn't get the message. My female organs shut down. I couldn't sleep. There were times when I stuttered and my speech was slurred. In my fear and torment over what had happened, I was tiresome around others. I did not comfort myself with food, but I sure looked like I did because my body bloated up from the stress.

Worst of all, God was silent. I would open my Bible and the words were pasted to the pages. They made no sense and gave no life. I would open my mouth to pray but nothing would come out. Sometimes I managed a few disjointed words, but it seemed as if they were snatched away as soon as they were uttered. After a while, I decided to just lie there with my mouth wide open and hope Someone was listening to the groanings that were too deep for uttering.

Down and down I went. A fast, accurate typist, I watched humbly as my fingers stumbled all over themselves as I transposed words and misspelled like crazy. I was frightened by my inability to remember important things and fearful about my inability to concentrate and problem-solve. I experienced panic attacks and had obsessive thoughts about frightening memories. Normally, I am a walker who enjoys the outdoors; now I sat day after day in my nightgown with the shades drawn. I love to laugh, yet I couldn't stop crying.

I couldn't get a grip, no matter how hard I tried. I was shut up and could not come forth. Finally, my husband said, "I'm taking you to see the doctor."

After listening to my list of symptoms, my doctor did another test and said, "Well, no wonder. It's all from the same source."

"What could that be?" I asked.

"Traumatic stress," she replied.

Post-Traumatic Stress Disorder

When you drop a rock into a pond, it only falls in one spot, but the ripples reach to the shore. In the same way, traumatic events only last for a short period of time, but the effects are far-reaching.

What's a trauma? A trauma is not merely being dissed and it's not an ordinary snubbing. Trauma occurs when what has happened to you is so far out of the normal range of experience that your world is turned upside-down.

Trauma has aspects of an ongoing sense of helplessness in the face of evil. For example, many of our schoolchildren are suffering from trauma in the wake of school shootings. They have absolutely no guarantee that their campus is not going to ring with gunshots, and so they go to school each day in a state of hyperarousal and anxiety.

Emotional reactions to severely traumatizing experiences include shock, confusion, helplessness, anxiety, fear, and depression. According to Dr. Rosemarie Amendolia, a fellow of the American Academy of Experts in Traumatic Stress, characteristic symptoms that may follow a psychologically traumatizing event include:

1. reexperiencing the traumatic event through repetitive, intrusive memories or recurring dreams
2. numbing or reduced responsiveness to the outside world
3. hyperarousal, including sleep disturbance, exaggerated startle response, and hypervigilance
4. avoidance of activities or inputs which cue recollections of the traumatic events.[1]

Because we live in a time when evil so often seems to overpower good, many of us are walking around in a chronic state of post-traumatic stress. Part of working through to forgiveness is tenderly healing your body, soul, and spirit of the wounds of trauma. My body needed extra nutrients, rest, and healing touch in order to heal. (Your doctor or counselor may have specific recommendations for you.) My soul has greatly benefited from counseling with someone who is trained to deal with traumatic stress. And, finally, I've cared for my spirit by climbing up into my Abba's lap and just letting Him hold me. For me, forgiveness has been a multi-faceted process which requires intentionality, patience, and outside help.

My prayer is that you, too, will find the resources to heal all three parts of your being. If you've been living in an abusive situation, you've probably had moments when you've been shocked and confused by your spouse's seeming inability to understand who you are and what you've just said. If you woke up one morning to discover the person you've been living with for the past twenty years has a secret life that is the exact opposite of his or her public life, that's very traumatic. In situations like these, your soul's going to need some extra attention.

Sometimes people are told they are codependent when what is really going on is they are showing symptoms of post-traumatic stress disorder. If you find yourself falling apart after a traumatic event, seek out those who are well-trained for counsel. Don't accept advice that only makes you feel worse than you already do. I recommend you find someone who is professionally trained and licensed. After many years of working with well-meaning but improperly trained counselors and finding their counsel often to be counterproductive and quite harmful, a year ago we started working with licensed professionals. There's been a *huge* difference in the healing we've experienced in our individual lives and in our home.[2]

Meanwhile, give your body some extra, tender loving care because stress really takes it out of you. Consider going for therapeutic massage. Pay attention to your diet and don't automatically say, "no" if your counselor suggests something to rebalance your brain's chemistry. Finally, develop your relationship with the One who is not only the Great Physician but also the Wonderful Counselor.

"And may the God of peace Himself sanctify you through and through; and may your spirit and soul and body be preserved sound and complete and found blameless at the coming of our Lord Jesus Christ."[3] Amen.

How to Discern Abusive Leadership

The Bible Teaches That:	Abusive Leaders Often Teach That:
you should die to your *sinful* desires.	you must die to *all* your desires.
God gives us the desires of our hearts.	to have desires is sinful.
only God knows the motivations of our heart.	they [leaders] know the thoughts and intents of our heart.
leaders must prove themselves to be trustworthy in order to be trusted.	leaders must be trusted because they are higher in the chain of command, and not to trust them is a sin.
leaders should show the virtues of Christ so that we can imitate those virtues.	you are out of "unity" if you disagree with the leader's opinions.
commitment to Jesus' ways is necessary.	commitment to obeying leaders is the same as commitment to Jesus.
you must obey *biblical* mandates.	you must obey the leader's opinions, even if your heart says *no*.
godly leaders are easy to approach and willing to hear what you have to say; it is OK to question.	refusal to see things their way is a sign of stubbornness and rebellion.

© There's Hope, P.O. Box 242, Cambridge, VT 05444

The Bible Teaches That:	Abusive Leaders Often Teach That:
leaders are held to a higher standard of accountability than those under them.	leaders are accountable only to God.
we have been delivered from shame.	shame keeps us in line; they use shame to intimidate.
godly leadership is servant leadership.	God has anointed them [leaders] to rule over us.
forgiveness and reconciliation are two different things.	you haven't forgiven if you're not willing to reconcile.
forgiveness is a free gift, but reconciliation with those who sin against you depends on their repentance.	it is controlling to expect repentance from others who have hurt you.
we reap what we sow, but sometimes bad things happen because someone else is out of control. Nevertheless, God is in control.	if bad things happen, it is because God is punishing you for hidden sin.
you should respect and help both the weak and people who are committed and strong.	you are wasting your time pouring yourself out to those who are uncommitted or lukewarm.
sometimes you have to shake the dust off your feet and move on.	leaving [their organization] puts you under the judgment of God.

© There's Hope, P.O. Box 242, Cambridge, VT 05444

The Bible Teaches That:	Abusive Leaders Often Teach That:
feelings are a normal part of human life, they are to be expressed in healthy ways and not denied.	negative feelings are to be denied; positive feelings may be suspect.
seeking justice is an important way to maintain the health of covenantal relationships.	asking for justice is being vindictive.
it is right to expect restitution when someone has stolen something that is ours.	asking for what belongs to you is a sign of selfishness.
individual property rights are to be honored, and personal boundaries are to be respected.	you have no rights, and boundaries are a sign of lack of submission.

Parts of this chart were adapted from
How to Discern Abusive Ministries
Control Techniques, Inc.
P.O. Box 8021
Chattanooga, TN 37414-8021

© There's Hope, P.O. Box 242, Cambridge, VT 05444

Recommended Reading

(The appearance of a book on this list doesn't necessarily mean I agree with everything in the book. It does mean that I've found the book extremely useful in my own journey of working through to forgiveness.)

Basics

Covey, Stephen R. *The Seven Habits of Highly Effective People.* New York: Simon and Schuster, 1989. Essential reading.

Elgin, Suzette Haden. *The Gentle Art of Verbal Self-Defense.* New York: Barnes & Noble, 1980. Very helpful.

Evans, Patricia. *The Verbally Abusive Relationship.* Holbrook, Mass.: Adams Media, 1996. Essential Reading.

Fisher, Roger, and William Ury. *Getting to Yes: Negotiating Agreement without Giving In.* New York: Penguin, 1991. Highly recommended.

Foster, Charles. *There's Something I Have to Tell You: How to Communicate Difficult News in Tough Situations.* New York: Harmony, 1997.

Lewis, David. *The Secret Language of Success: Using Body Language to Get What You Want.* New York: Galahad, 1989.

Nierenberg, Gerard I., and Henry H. Calero. *How to Read a Person Like a Book.* New York: Barnes and Noble, 1993.

Fasting and Prayer

Blauer, Stephen. *The Juicing Book*. Garden City Park, New York: Avery, 1989.

Eastman, Dick, and Jack Hayford. *Living and Praying in Jesus' Name*. Wheaton, Ill.: Tyndale House, 1988.

Greig, Gary S., and Kevin N. Springer, eds. *The Kingdom and the Power*. Ventura, Calif.: Regal, 1993.

Nouwen, Henri J.M. *The Way of the Heart*. New York: Ballantine, 1981.

Nouwen, Henri J.M. *With Open Hands*. Notre Dame, Ind.: Ave Maria Press, 1972.

Rhodes, Tricia McCary. *The Soul at Rest*. Minneapolis, Minn.: Bethany, 1996. This is a wonderful book. Every time I pick up my copy, I can feel my soul breathing a sigh of relief. Highly recommended.

Towns, Elmer L. *Fasting for Spiritual Breakthrough*. Ventura, Calif.: Regal, 1996.

Addictions

Bergner, Mario. *Setting Love in Order*. Grand Rapids, Mich.: Baker Books, 1995.

Hall, Laurie. *An Affair of the Mind*. Wheaton, Ill.: Tyndale /Focus on the Family, 1996.

Laaser, Mark. *Faithful and True: Sexual Integrity in a Fallen World*. Grand Rapids, Mich.: Zondervan, 1992.

Nakken, Craig. *The Addictive Personality*. Center City, Minn.: Hazeldon, 1996.

Payne, Leanne. *The Broken Image.* Wheaton, Ill.: Crossway Books, 1981. Anything Leanne writes is highly recommended.

Worthen, Anita, and Bob Davies. *Someone I Love Is Gay.* Downers Grove, Ill.: InterVarsity, 1996.

Healing the Soul

Allender, Dan B., and Tremper Longman III. *Bold Love.* Colorado Springs: NavPress, 1992. Essential reading.

Bonhoeffer, Dietrich. *Creation and Fall/ Temptation: Two Biblical Studies.* New York: Simon & Schuster, 1983.

Bunyan, John. *The Pilgrim's Progress.* (Many editions)

Canfield, Ken. *The Seven Secrets of Effective Fathers.* Wheaton, Ill.: Tyndale House Publishers, 1995.

_____. *The Heart of a Father.* Chicago: Northfield Publications, 1996.

Kreeft, Peter. *Making Sense out of Suffering.* Ann Arbor, Mich.: Servant Books, 1986.

Linn, Dennis, Sheila Fabricant Linn, and Matthew Linn, S.J. *Don't Forgive Too Soon.* New York: Paulist, 1997. Essential reading.

Payne, Leanne. *The Healing Presence: Curing the Soul through Union with Christ.* Grand Rapids, Mich.: Baker Books, 1995.

_____. *Restoring the Christian Soul: Overcoming Barriers to Completion in Christ Through Healing Prayer.* Grand Rapids, Mich.: Baker, 1996.

Pearsall, Paul. *The Heart's Code: New Findings About Cellular Memories and Their Role in the Mind/Body/Spirit Connection.* New York: Broadway, 1998. I thought a long time before recommending this book because some of the information is a bit New Age, but the medical information is so very helpful. I trust your judgment to sift through it.

Seamands, David A. *Healing for Damaged Emotions.* Wheaton, Ill.: Victor, 1988.

Smedes, Lewis B. *The Art of Forgiving: When You Need to Forgive and Don't Know How.* New York: Random House, 1996.

von Hildebrand, Dietrich. *Making Christ's Peace Part of Your Life.* Manchester, N.H.: Sophia Institute Press, 1998.

West, Kari, and Noelle Quinn. *When He Leaves.* Colorado Springs: Chariot Victor, 1998.

About Covenant

Intrater, Keith. *Covenant Relationships.* Shippensburg, Penn.: Destiny Image, 1989.

Poythress, Vern S. *The Shadow of Christ in the Law of Moses.* Phillipsburg, N.J.: Presbyterian and Reformed Publishing, 1991.

Richards, Larry. *Every Covenant and Promise in the Bible.* Nashville: Thomas Nelson, 1998.

Wead, Doug, David Lewis, and Hal Donaldson. *Where Is the Lost Ark?* Minneapolis, Minn.: Bethany, 1982.

On the Sanctity of the Counseling Relationship

Chrnalogar, Mary Alice. *Twisted Scriptures: A Path to Freedom from Abusive Churches.* Chattanooga, Tenn.: Control Techniques, 1997. Order directly from Mary Alice, 1-423-698-9343.

Fortune, Marie M. *Is Nothing Sacred?* San Francisco: HarperCollins, 1989.

Labacqz, Karen, and Ronald G. Barton. *Sex in the Parish.* Louisville, Ky.: John Knox, 1991.

Peterson, Marilyn R. *At Personal Risk: Boundary Violations in Professional-Client Relationships.* New York: W.W. Norton, 1992. Essential reading.

Rutter, Peter M., M.D. *Sex in the Forbidden Zone.* New York: Fawcett Columbine, 1989. Essential reading.

NOTES

Chapter 1
Change Is Inevitable, Except From a Vending Machine

1. Sg 2:10-13.

Chapter 2
You Can't Get There From Here

1. Michael and Angeline Rogers, both twenty-nine, were convicted of locking their seven-year-old daughter in a dog cage and beating four of their five children with sticks and pipes.

2. The judge was Philadelphia Court of Common Pleas Judge Frederica Massiah-Jackson, who, in spite of a dismal record of failing to uphold the rights of victims, was nominated by President Clinton to a lifetime appointment as a federal judge. Strong opposition forced the judge to decline her nomination. From Daniel Levine, "America's Worst Judges," *Reader's Digest,* September 1998, 81.

3. Ron Stodghill, "Where Did You Learn That?" *Time,* June 15, 1998 (Vol. 151, No. 23), 52–59. Quoted in *Current Thoughts and Trends,* September 1998, 11.

4. The figure is from 1996. "Pastor's Weekly Briefing," August 29, 1997, quoted in *Current Thoughts and Trends,* December 1997, 6.

5. Judith Havemann, "A Nation of Violent Children," *Washington Post Weekly,* February 17, 1997 (Vol. 14, No. 16), 24.

6. *Youthworker Update,* March 1997, 7. Fatherlessness is devastating for children. Researchers at Rutgers University have documented that children living in a traditional home with both mother and father receive more emotional support than children who live only with their mother. "By measuring the quality of the home environment (according to the modified Home Observation for Measurement, or HOME, scale) the amount of emotional support children could expect was related to whether or not their father lived in the same home as the mother. The researchers found that children from middle-income fami-

lies with married mothers scored on average 28 percentiles higher on the emotional support scale than their peers whose mothers were divorced or of other marital status. For the children of divorce the cause of this emotional support deficit was due to their less frequent contact with fathers, according to the study." "The Family in America," *New Research*, March 1998. Quoted in *AFA Journal*, September 1998, 9.

7. Quoted in *Current Thoughts and Trends*, September 1998, 12.
8. *USA Today*, July 31, 1998. *AFA Journal*, September 1998, 9.
9. "Kids Who Kill Kids," *Current Thoughts and Trends*, October 1997, 10.
10. *Emerging Trends*, March 1997, 5. Quoted in *Current Thoughts and Trends*, June 1997, 9.
11. "Who Influences Teens?" *AFA Journal*, September 1998, 8.
12. "Pastor's Weekly Briefing," July 3, 1998, 2. Quoted in *Current Thoughts and Trends*, September 1998, 9.
13. Deborah Blum, "Finding Strength," *Psychology Today*, May-June 1998 (Vol. 31, No. 3), 32–38. Quoted in *Current Thoughts and Trends*, September 1998, 14.

Chapter 3
I Tried Walking on Water Once and It Didn't Go Well

1. Gilbert Meilander, *First Things*, June-July 1998, reprinted in *American Family Association Journal*, September 1998, 16.
2. See Lk 23:34; 1 Cor 15:3, 4; 1 Jn 1:9.
3. See Rom 12:2; 2 Cor 5:17; Heb 7:25.
4. Meilander, 16.
5. Micah 6:8 says, "He has shown thee, O man, what is good and what the Lord requires of thee, but to do justly, and to love mercy, and to walk humbly with thy God."
6. Heb 12:5a, AMPLIFIED.
7. See Jn 8:11.
8. See Mt 23:27.
9. See Jn 2:15.
10. Jn 15:13, 14.
11. See Rom 5:8, 10.

Chapter 4
The Emperor Has No Clothes

1. John Dillenberger, *Martin Luther: Selections from His Writings* (New York: Doubleday, 1962), 45.

2. *Insight,* January 5, 1998, 35, quoted in *Current Thoughts and Trends,* August 1998, 24.

3. *Religion Watch,* May 1997, 4.

4. Figures taken from Justin Long, "North America: Decline and Fall of World Religions, 1900-2025," *Monday Morning Reality Check,* February 23, 1998, 1–3.

5. Long, 3.

6. George Barna, "Has Revival Begun?" *Barna Report,* 1997 (Vol. 1, No. 6), 1-5.

7. Barna, 1-5.

8. George Barna, "The Faith of Men," *Barna Report,* 1997 (Vol. 1, No. 5), 4-6. Quoted in *Current Thoughts and Trends,* June 1997, 21.

9. Barna, 1-5.

10. Dennis Rainey, "Danger in the Middle," *Moody,* November-December 1998 (Vol. 99, No. 12), 38-40. Quoted in *Current Thoughts and Trends,* February 1999, 12.

11. Robert T. Michael, et al., *Sex in America: A Definitive Survey* (Boston: Little, Brown, 1994).

12. I prefer the term sexual brokenness because I feel it better describes the condition than "sexual sin." I define sexual brokenness as a perversion of the good gift of sexuality in which a man uses sex as an agent for power over others or as a way to numb inner pain or as a "magic carpet" to provide temporary relief from the pressures of life.

13. Julia Duin, "Churches Fight Sin Within Their Ranks," *Washington Times,* February 25, 1999.

14. Ken Abraham, "Exposing Domestic Violence," *New Man,* May 1998 (Vol. 5, No. 3), 34ff. Quoted in *Current Thoughts and Trends,* July 1998, 11.

15. Denyse O'Leary, "Divorce: Can We Do Better?" *Faith Today,* Nov-Dec 1998 (Vol. 16, No. 6), 20–27. Quoted in *Current Thoughts and Trends,* February 1999, 9.

Chapter 5

When the Prince You're Kissing Turns Into a Frog

1. Rom 7:10.
2. Prv 14:12.
3. Jer 17:9.
4. Rom 1:19-32, AMPLIFIED.
5. See Jn 8:32.
6. Jas 1:2-4, AMPLIFIED.
7. 1 Pt 1:6, 7, AMPLIFIED.

Chapter 6

Some Drink at the Fountain of Knowledge; Others Only Gargle

1. Peter Kreeft, *Making Sense Out of Suffering* (Ann Arbor, Mich.: Servant, 1986), 58.
2. While I understand what Kreeft is saying here, I think believing there are no answers is the most dogmatic kind of "answer."
3. Kreeft, 29.
4. See 2 Cor 10:5.
5. Nancy Gibbs, "The Star Report," *Time,* September 21, 1998, 35.
6. 1 Cor 2:15, 16, AMPLIFIED.
7. Ez 37:1-3, AMPLIFIED.
8. See Is 40:4.
9. See Ps 23; Dt 33:27.

Chapter 7

Dust: Mud With the Juice Squeezed Out

1. Leo Tolstoy, *A Confession* (London: Penguin, 1987), 66.
2. For those who are wondering about my insertion of the word "together" in the Gn 1:28 passage, the text clearly says that God gave the command unto *them.*
3. Thinking that someone is messing with Scripture can cause us to hyperventilate. So, for those of you who are saying, "I've never read Creation in this order before," I will explain what I've done: I have woven the text of Genesis

1 and 2, Hebrews 1, and John 1:1-5 together. I think it is possible to look at the text the way one would look at the map of a state. You have the overview of the state, showing the location of all the cities, but then you have certain important cities that are taken out and "blown up" so you can see the details. In the same way, I think God describes the creation of man. He gives the overview in Gn 1:27-30, but more specific details in Gn 2:7-25. I think it's *possible* that the actual order of Creation might have gone something like this: Gn 1:1-27, Gn 2:7-9, Gn 2:15-22, Gn 1:28-31, Gn 2:23-24, and I have reflected that in this rendition. We weren't privileged to be there; we can only do our best to try to understand the text without changing it.

Those of you who may wonder where I got phrases such as the Tree of the Knowledge of the Difference Between that Which is Excellent, Beautiful, and Cheerful, and that Which is Mischievous, Malignant, and Deadly should know that such expansions of a word or phrase come from their meanings in Hebrew. In Hebrew, "good" means that which is excellent, beautiful, and cheerful. Throughout my Creation account, I have plugged in only what the original Hebrew says.

4. Dr. Henry Blackaby, in a speech entitled "What Do You See as the Future for the United States?" Billy Graham Training Center, Asheville, N.C., May 22, 1999.

5. O'Leary, 20–27.

6. The statistics on the general population come from *Sex in America: A Definitive Survey.* The statistics on the church come from surveys done by the National Center for Fathering at Promise Keepers arena events and by Dr. Archibald Hart for "Men and Sex in the 90s." I have chosen not to name a percentage for the pastors because I don't know of any study that specifically asks pastors about their involvement with porn. However, I have been given a percentage figure by a number of different people who work with pastors and who have their hands on the pulse of what is happening with church leaders, people who come from across the United States and who all gave me the same figure without consulting each other. I will tell you that it was a much higher figure than the one for the man in the pew.

7. Mt 7:17-18, 20, AMPLIFIED.

8. Introductory comments on the Book of Genesis, *The Amplified Bible* (Grand Rapids, Mich.: Zondervan, 1987), 1.

9. Stars are about 97% hydrogen and helium and 3% argon, carbon, chlorine, iron, magnesium, neon, nitrogen, oxygen, silicon, sulfur, and other elements. Some stars send out strong radio waves, others send out x-rays, and still others

212 / The Cleavers Don't Live Here Anymore

send out mainly heat. There are blue stars, white stars, orange stars, yellow stars, and red stars. There are main-sequence stars, giant and supergiant stars, white dwarfs, variable stars, binary stars, quasars, and mystery stars. There are very, very bright stars and very, very dim stars.

10. Maybe you've tried this formula with variations on the theme. Perhaps you haven't gone the domestic goddess route of homeschooling, but you've found other ways to be actively involved in your children's education.

11. Lk 22:25-26.

Chapter 8
Fig Leaves Are Us

1. Watchman Nee, *The Spiritual Man* (New York: Christian Fellowship Publishers, Inc., 1977), Vol. 11, 85.

2. The word for good could be translated "moral good" and the word for evil could be translated "moral deficiency."

3. 1 Cor 10:29, AMPLIFIED.

4. See 1 Tm 2:14.

5. Hebrews 4:12-16 dovetails with this thought.

6. Accountability for time and money spent is not necessarily a bad thing. Indeed, behavior modification is an important part of breaking free of addictions. However, this church's total approach to healing was to shame Marc into better behavior. They naively thought that if they could keep him from the opportunity to sin, they could somehow extinguish in him the desire to do so. They missed the fact that his outward behavior was a symptom of a broken soul, and they absolutely did not know how to go into the brokenness of his lonely soul and speak life. They only knew how to control. In a healthy accountability relationship, we do right not because we are being watched but because we are being loved.

7. Rom 13:8.

Chapter 9
After This, All the Rest Is Just Details

1. See Mt 20:23, 25-28.

2. Jn 14:2.

3. See Heb 1:2-3.

4. See Gn 1:15.

5. Gn 1:28, AMPLIFIED.

6. Eph 4:11-13, AMPLIFIED.

7. Spiro Zodhiates, *Greek Hebrew Study Bible* (Grand Rapids, Mich.: Baker, 1984), 1583.

8. See Mt 3:17; 12:18; 17:5.

9. This story is told in Numbers 16 and 17.

10. See Ez 19:11-12, 14.

11. Jn 15:5 [brackets mine].

12. See Acts 2:43; 3:6; 4:30; 5:12; 8:13; 12:6-10; 14:3; 19:11; Ro 15:19.

13. Jn 6:49-50 [brackets mine].

14. Heb 9:1–10:39.

15. Mt 6:9-13, AMPLIFIED [brackets mine].

16. Jn 14:13–15.

17. The story is told in 1 Samuel 4-7.

18. See Heb 7:25.

Chapter 10
Grumble, Grumble, Beans, Burgers, and Trouble

1. Dietrich Bonhoeffer, *The Cost of Discipleship* (New York: Macmillan, 1978), 24.

2. See Eph 1:4.

3. Phil 7:5-7.

4. See Ex 16:1-36.

5. An omer is not quite a gallon, about 3 1/2 quarts.

6. Jn 6:48-51.

Chapter 11
Lessons From the School of Abandonment

1. Henri J. M. Nouwen, *With Open Hands* (Notre Dame, Ind.: Ave Maria, 1972), 95.

2. You can read this story for yourself in Genesis 37-50.

3. The King James translates Mark 15:34, "My God, my God, why hast thou forsaken me?" The Greek word for "forsaken" means "to leave in the lurch." The Greek word for "cry" means "to cry out with fear and terror."

4. *The Amplified Bible* (Grand Rapids, Mich.: Zondervan, 1964), footnote to Ps 22.

5. Ps 22:1-2, 4-8, 14-15, AMPLIFIED.
6. Mk 15:37.
7. I am grateful to my friend Janet Franklin for this insight.
8. Barbara Brown Taylor, *Home by Another Way* (Cambridge, Mass.: Crowley Publications, 1999), 43.
9. Dietrich Bonhoeffer, *Creation and Fall/ Temptation: Two Biblical Studies* (New York: Simon & Schuster, 1997), 111-12.

Chapter 12
Got Bread?

1. Marie M. Fortune, *Is Nothing Sacred?* (San Francisco: HarperCollins, 1989), 114, 160.
2. For you animal lovers, this biting and kicking wasn't constant, but it was intentional until the pecking order was established.
3. This phrase came from my friend Janet Franklin, who helped me understand the kicking and biting syndrome.
4. Patricia Evans, *The Verbally Abusive Relationship* (Holbrook, Mass.: Adams Media Corporation, 1996), 37.
5. Acts 1:7. There are many other places where Jesus tells His disciples they have the power and authority necessary to do their jobs. Luke 10:17-20; Mark 6:7 among others.
6. Phil 2:5-7a.
7. Evans, 65.
8. Rom 12:17, 19-21, AMPLIFIED.
9. 1 Jn 3:1-2.
10. 1 Jn 3:3.
11. Col 1:27.
12. Jn 15:15.
13. Jn 16:15, AMPLIFIED.

Chapter 13
Abigail's Legacy

1. Ann Brener, *Mourning & Mitzvah* (Woodstock, Vt.: Jewish Lights, 1993), 4.
2. This story is told in 1 Samuel 25.
3. See Mt 4:5-7.

4. In Genesis 1:28, God commands Adam and Eve to take dominion: to be fruitful, multiply, and subdue the earth.
5. See 1 Pt 3:1-6.
6. Marie Powers, *Shame, Thief of Intimacy* (Lynnwood, Wash.: Aglow International, 1996), 22.
7. See Rom 8:1; Jn 3:17; Is 59:4-7, 61:7-8.
8. Chris Newton, "Student Sues School Over Scandalous Photo of Principal" (*Burlington* [Vt] *Free Press*, September 11, 1999), 13A.
9. Dan Allender and Tremper Longman, *Bold Love* (Colorado Springs: NavPress, 1992), 238.
10. Fortune, 120.
11. Fortune, 120.

Chapter 14
When Paradigms Shift, Gears Grind

1. Dennis Linn, Sheila Fabricant Linn, and Matthew Linn, *Don't Forgive Too Soon* (New York: Paulist, 1997), 120.
2. Lk 4:18-19, AMPLIFIED.
3. Linn, 8.
4. Spiro Zodhiates, *The Complete Word Study Dictionary, New Testament* (Chattanooga, Tenn.: AMG Publishers, 1992), 405.
5. Linn, 5.
6. Linn, 5.
7. This story is told again in Luke 6:29-30 and the two accounts differ as to what the poor man is required to hand over. In the Luke passage, he was required to hand over his "himation," or outer cloak, first, which corresponds to the instructions in Exodus 22:25-27 that specify the outer cloak's use as collateral for a loan. In Matthew's account, he must hand over his "chiton," or underwear, first. Whichever the poor man gave up first, the result is the same—he was naked.
8. Linn, 7.
9. Linn, 7.
10. Mt 26:27-28, AMPLIFIED.
11. This idea came from Rev. Henry MacLeod, rector of St. James Episcopal Church in Essex Junction, Vt.
12. Prv 25:21-22.

13. Heb 12:2, AMPLIFIED.
14. Mt 17:5.
15. Mt 3:17.

Chapter 15
The Gates Are Down, the Lights Are Flashing,
but the Train Is Nowhere in Sight

1. Nouwen, 12.
2. Lk 4:18-19, AMPLIFIED.
3. Ez 36:26-29a, AMPLIFIED.
4. Ps 19:7, AMPLIFIED.
5. Ex 25:22. This passage speaks of the Ark of the Covenant. In the Old Covenant, the Ark dwelt in the Tabernacle, also known as the "tent of the congregation" because the Lord met His people there. It was to be filled with the glory of the Lord. By His presence there He would personally lead the children of Israel on their journey. (Baker Zodhiates, *The Greek-Hebrew Study Bible,* 112.)
   In the New Testament, we *become* the tabernacle of God. It is Christ in me the hope of glory. He says, "My sheep hear my voice and I know them and show them all that the Father is doing."
6. Throughout my discussion of faith, hope, and love, I will be using some thoughts Dan Allender presented at a workshop given at the 1997 World Congress of the American Association for Christian Counselors in Dallas, Texas.
7. Kreeft, 155.
8. I borrowed this phrase from Dan Allender.
9. Dan Allender says that nostalgia is airbrushing reality.
10. Ps 77:3, AMPLIFIED.
11. "Ginny Helfrich, a nationally certified chemical dependency counselor in Seattle, has found that teaching people to 'sound' the emotions they feel—and thereby listen to their unresolved pain—makes it easier for them to connect with issues surrounding their addiction. 'Often these unresolved issues have plagued them for many years,' she says, 'and they have tried to medicate their inner pain with drugs, alcohol, overeating, or various denial or transference behaviors or attitudes. Having expressed locked-up negative emotions, they can move on to develop more positive and healthy ways of living.'" Don

Campbell, *The Mozart Effect* (New York: Avon Books, 1997), 274.

12. I have adapted this thought from Dan Allender.
13. Jer 29:11, AMPLIFIED.
14. Mt 24:12, AMPLIFIED.
15. See James 1:8.
16. See Mt 22:37-39.
17. 1 Jn 4:16. Actually, the entire book of 1 John teaches this.
18. 1 Cor 13:13.

Chapter 16
Growing Flowers on the Manure Piles of Life

1. See Jn 2:24-25.
2. Jn 6:37, AMPLIFIED.
3. Jn 6:35, AMPLIFIED.
4. See Heb 12:2-4, AMPLIFIED.
5. Jn 16:13 and 1 Cor 2:15-16, AMPLIFIED.
6. See Gn 3:15.
7. Jn 3:16-18, Acts 4:12, AMPLIFIED.

Epilogue
One Last Thing ...

1. http://www.aaets.org
2. I know. This type of counseling is not cheap. Insurance may cover part of the cost and many therapists have a sliding fee. Just because someone is licensed doesn't mean he or she is the right counselor for you. Interview the counselor. Ask if he or she has specialized training in the area where you need help. See if you feel comfortable together. A good counselor helps you re-establish your personal boundaries. You should feel respected and listened to in your counseling sessions.
3. 1 Thes 5:23, AMPLIFIED.

Laurie Hall welcomes your inquiries
regarding speaking engagements. She
can be contact at:

P.O. Box 242
Cambridge, Vt 05444

———

To receive *There's Hope* newsletter, please write to
P.O. Box 242, Cambridge, VT, 05444.
Annual subscription rate is $20.
Please make checks payable to The Elijah Initiative.